365

GOLF TIPS
& TRICKS
FROM THE PROS

365

GOLF TIPS
& TRICKS

FROM THE PROS

EDITED BY JAY MORELLI,

Director of The Original Golf School

PHOTOGRAPHY BY BRUCE CURTIS

STERLING
New York

STERLING
New York

An Imprint of Sterling Publishing
387 Park Avenue South
New York, NY 10016

STERLING and the distinctive Sterling logo are registered trademarks of Sterling Publishing Co., Inc.

Photo credits:
Page 453: courtesy of Shutterstock Images LLC ©Val Thoermer
Page 551: courtesy of Shutterstock Images LLC ©janprchal

ISBN 978-1-4027-8813-0

Library of Congress Cataloging-in-Publication Data

365 golf tips & tricks from the pros / edited by Jay Morelli; photography by Bruce Curtis.
   p. cm.
  Includes index.
  ISBN 978-1-4027-8813-0 (pbk.) – ISBN 978-1-4027-9380-6 (ebook)
  1. Golf–Handbooks, manuals, etc. I. Morelli, Jay. II. Title: Three hundred sixty-five golf tips and tricks
from the pros.
  GV965.A18 2013
  796.352'3–dc23

2012019262

Distributed in Canada by Sterling Publishing
c/o Canadian Manda Group, 165 Dufferin Street
Toronto, Ontario, Canada M6K 3H6
Distributed in the United Kingdom by GMC Distribution Services
Castle Place, 166 High Street, Lewes, East Sussex, England BN7 1XU
Distributed in Australia by Capricorn Link (Australia) Pty. Ltd.
P.O. Box 704, Windsor, NSW 2756, Australia

For information about custom editions, special sales, and premium and
corporate purchases, please contact Sterling Special Sales at 800-805-5489
or specialsales@sterlingpublishing.com.

Manufactured in China

2 4 6 8 10 9 7 5 3 1

www.sterlingpublishing.com

CONTENTS

St Andrews Links

The largest golf comple...

Six public cou...

Two clubho...

Golf practice...

Three sh...

Information and offic...

www.standrew...

Book golf directly at
top courses in Scotland and
around the world
by using

www.golfagent.co...

St Andrews Li...

Pilmou...

St Andrews...

Fife KY16 9...

Telephone (0)133...

Fax (0)1334...

Hole	Marker's Score	Name	White Yards	Par	
1		BOATHOUSE	328	4	
2		OWER THE KNOWE	494	5	
3		THE BRIGGS	184	3	
4		FLUKE DUB	346	4	3
5		HELL'S HOLE	459	4	4
		WORMISTON	186	3	17
		NORTH CARR	349	4	288
		BREECHES B...	442	4	425
		DYKESID...	306	4	253
		OUT	3094	35 / 34	2841

CE...OTS, REPAIR PITCHM...

		...E YETTS	336	4	287
12		...NG WHANG	496	4	428
1...		...THE BURN	528	5	519
		CRAIGHEAD	219	3	208
		THE CAVE	150	3	140
...6		MILL DAM	270	4	260
17		SPION KOP	163	3	156
18		ROAD HOLE	463	4	418
		THE QUARRY	203	3	196
		IN	2828	34 / 33	2612
		OUT	3094	35 / 34	2841
		TOTAL	5922	69 / 67	5453

STABLEFORD
POINTS OR
PAR RESULT

HAN...

INTRODUCTION

Golf is a sport that requires knowledge as well as good fundamentals. I feel the most valuable knowledge can be gained from the PGA teaching pros at the golf schools across the country. At school, you live and breathe golf. You receive good information and swing corrections as well as positive reinforcement. This total-immersion approach increases a player's understanding of the game, and there is no substitute for a very good teacher, whether in a private lesson or at a golf school. So I've gathered 365 of the most valuable tips from more than sixty of the most talented and knowledgeable teaching pros in the United States, along with others with insight into the game, and put them in this book. From knowing the rule book and the etiquette of the game to chip shots, sand play, putting, and more, 365 *Golf Tips & Tricks from the Pros* gives you the hands-on tips and advice from the pros who make thousands of golfers each year better at their game. Now it's your turn.

—*Jay Morelli, Director of the Original Golf School*

GOLF RULES

1 THE RULE BOOK

Kate Baker, LPGA Teaching Pro, Pebble Beach, California, and the Greens at Half Hollow, Melville, New York

It's important to play by the United States Golf Association (USGA) *Rules of Golf*. The *Rules of Golf* are the only way you can accurately determine your score. If you play fast and loose with the rules, you'll never know if your game has improved. Adhering to the rules gives you an accurate barometer of your game. You can purchase an official rule book from the USGA at www.usga.org/PublicationsStore/. Remember that there are more "free lifts" in the rules than there are penalties.

2 OWN A RULE BOOK
Kate Baker, LPGA Teaching Pro, Pebble Beach, California, and the
Greens at Half Hollow, Melville, New York

The best advice I can give is to have a copy of the USGA's *Rules of Golf* in your bag. Somewhere along the way you will be in a competition with someone who is, or thinks he is, a rules expert. If a violation is called on you, the best move is to take out the *Rules of Golf* and have him point out the infraction to you. If he is correct, you learn something. If you are correct, he learns something and you save a few strokes.

3 LEARN THE RULES
Kate Baker, LPGA Teaching Pro, Pebble Beach, California, and the
Greens at Half Hollow, Melville, New York

The *Rules of Golf* may not be the most interesting reading in the world, but it's a worthwhile investment of your time and money. To learn quickly, read the "Definitions" and "Etiquette" sections. They are the basis of the *Rules of Golf*. If you understand these sections, you will be far ahead of golfers who have played for years.

USGA

2010 – 2011
The Rules of Golf

And the Rules of Amateur Status

4 HOW GOLF RULES EVOLVED
Kate Baker, LPGA Teaching Pro, Pebble Beach, California, and the Greens at Half Hollow, Melville, New York

In the early days of golf, all play was match play. One player or team played against another player or team. Rules did not have to be consistent, as their play would not affect other players on the course. As competition changed to medal or stroke play, rules had to be consistent. The playing field had to be level. The player with an 8:00 tee-off time had to play under the same conditions as the player who had a 10:00 tee-off time.

5 ONE CLUB LENGTH OR TWO?
Kate Baker, LPGA Teaching Pro, Pebble Beach, California, and the Greens at Half Hollow, Melville, New York

Sometimes we are entitled to free relief (moving or dropping the ball away from an obstruction without incurring a penalty); other times the ball is in a hazard and we choose to drop from the hazard. Simply put, the rule is that when we are taking free relief, such as from casual water or from a cart path, we get relief and one club length. When we have to take a penalty stroke, we get two club lengths from the margin of the hazard.

6 WHERE DO I DROP FROM A LATERAL WATER HAZARD?

Mark Brown, PGA Director of Golf, Tam O'Shanter Club, Brookville, New York

Lateral water hazards are marked by red stakes or paint. There are actually five options:

1. Play the ball as it lies.
2. Play the ball under the penalty of stroke and distance.
3. Drop behind the hazard where the ball last crossed the margin of the hazard line, keeping that point in line with the hole with no limit to how far behind that point the ball may be dropped.
4. Drop within two club lengths from the point of entry into the hazard.
5. Drop two club lengths from the opposite margin, equidistant from the hole.

7 RELIEF FROM IMMOVABLE OBSTRUCTIONS

Kate Baker, LPGA Teaching Pro, Pebble Beach, California, and the Greens at Half Hollow, Melville, New York

An immovable obstruction is an artificial or human-made object you cannot move. You get relief if the immovable obstruction interferes with your stance or swing. To take relief, find the nearest point where the obstruction does not interfere with your swing or stance. Drop the ball within one club length of that point, no closer to the hole. You must take complete relief from the obstruction.

8 HOW DO I DROP FROM AN UNPLAYABLE LIE?

Stevie Hovey, Rules Expert, the Original Golf School,
Mount Snow, Vermont

The player may deem the ball unplayable at any place on the course except when the ball is in a water hazard. The player is the sole judge. If the player deems the ball unplayable, he or she must, under penalty of one stroke:

1. Play from the spot where the original ball was last played.
2. Drop behind the point where the ball lies, keeping that point between the ball and the hole with no limit as to how far behind that point the ball may be dropped.
3. Drop within two club lengths of where the ball lies, not nearer the hole.

9 THE MOST MISUNDERSTOOD RULE IN GOLF—THE LOST BALL

Mark Brown, PGA Director of Golf, Tam O'Shanter Club,
Brookville, New York

There is only one option if you lose your ball, and that is to return to where you hit the ball from and replay the stroke under the penalty of stroke and distance. If you lose your tee shot, the only option is to go back to the tee. You will then be playing your third shot. While this is according to the rules, many courses will treat the tree line as a lateral hazard, so your best option is to drop the ball at the point of entry with a one-stroke penalty. A good practice, and one that is correct according to the rules, is to play a "provisional ball" if you think your ball has been lost. This saves time and is the correct procedure.

10 RELIEF FROM CASUAL WATER
Shari Pfannenstein, PGA Rules Expert

A player receives relief from casual water if it interferes with the player's stance or swing. Casual water is water that has accumulated that is not part of a hazard. The procedure is to take the nearest relief no closer to the hole. (And remember there is only one "nearest.") Mark the ball's location with a tee. Once relief has been taken, measure one club length from the ball, again not nearer the hole, and mark that point with a tee. You may drop the ball between the tees and proceed with no penalty. Remember, you *do not* have to play from puddles or accumulated water on the course that is not part of a hazard.

11 HANDICAP

Jay Morelli, Director of the Original Golf School,
Mount Snow, Vermont

A *handicap* in golf is the number of strokes you score over par on a fairly good day. If a player has a 20 handicap, that means he will score about 92 on a par-72 course. The concept of a handicap is that it is a method of leveling the playing field so two players of different abilities can engage in a fair competition. A 10-handicap player would give the 20-handicap player one stroke on the ten most difficult holes. (The 20-handicap player would deduct one stroke on each of those ten most difficult holes.) The handicap is determined by a computerized system through the USGA.

Overall points score

er. Gary Lisbon Handicap. 6

ner. Peter McKinnon Handicap 18

2 April 2002 Home Club.
The National Golf Club

npetition Stableford

C.C.R.
38

ndex	Player		+ o	Marker	+ o	Hole	Metres	Metres	Par	Index	Player		+ o	Marker
10	4	2				10	374	356	4	9	3	3		
14	5	2				11	359	334	4	13	3	3		Course
6	6	1		Birdie on a		12	532	510	5	7	4	3		rating f
1	3	(4)		Par 4 with a		13	170	159	3	18	4	1		the day
12	4	1		stroke = net		14	422	420	4	5	4	3		
4	4	3		eagle (4 points)		15	524	495	5	11	5	2		
8	6	1				16	447	422	4	2	4	3		
17	3	2				17	204	170	3	15	5	(-)		← Double bo
16	5	1				18	412	387	4	3	5	2		on Par 3 v
	40	17				In	3444	3253	36		37	20		no stroke
						Out	3132	2939	36		40	17		0 points
						Total	6576	6192	72		77	37		
						Less Handicap								
						NET TOTAL								

No. of points
based on score
and rating of hole

Points Scoring : D/Bogey = 0 points, Bogey = 1
Par = 2, Birdie = 3, Eagle = 4, Albatross = 5

12 SHOTGUN TOURNAMENT
Jay Morelli, Director of the Original Golf School,
Mount Snow, Vermont

A *shotgun tournament* is one where the entire field tees off at the same time. The players start on all or almost all the holes on the course. The advantage to that style of tournament is that all players begin and end the round at the same time. The disadvantage is that it is more difficult for the course to provide the best service, as every player is starting and ending at the same time. Another disadvantage is that some players will start on easy holes, others on difficult holes. The course architect almost always starts the course with a moderate or easy hole to get you started.

13 SCRAMBLE TOURNAMENT
Jay Morelli, Director of the Original Golf School,
Mount Snow, Vermont

The *scramble* is a team of two to four players. Everyone tees off and then the best of the tee shots is chosen. All players then play their second shots from that spot. This continues until a ball is holed. Each hole is played that way and eventually you post a score. This format is often called a *best ball* tournament. There is a tournament called a "best ball," but that follows a different format. The scramble format is good for when the field has a mix of experienced and new golfers.

14 BEST BALL TOURNAMENT

Jay Morelli, Director of the Original Golf School,
Mount Snow, Vermont

A best ball team is made up of two to four players. Each player plays out the hole. The best single score of the players is recorded. If one player scores a three and the other players make eights, the three is the team score. The collective score of the eighteen holes is the team score. This is a good format when all players are experienced.

15 PRO-AM

*Jay Morelli, Director of the Original Golf School,
Mount Snow, Vermont*

A Pro-Am is a tournament with both professional and amateur golfers comprising each team. The standard format is one professional and three amateurs, but it can be any combination. In most of the Pro-Ams, the amateur will receive a handicap. There are countless ways to keep score, but, suffice to say, it's a great way for the amateurs to play with the pros. The best-known Pro-Am is the Pebble Beach National Pro-Am, which is a professional golf tournament on the PGA Tour held every year on three different courses. The event was originally known as the Bing Crosby National Pro-Amateur, or just the Crosby Clambake.

16 THE NINETEENTH HOLE
Bruce Curtis, photographer and former bartender, the Pepsi Café, Saigon, Vietnam, 1968

The nineteenth hole is as much a part of golf as the previous eighteen. It is the place where you settle up the Nassau (a match-play wager), or order the twenty-five-year-old scotch whiskey because that lucky so-and-so got a hole in one on the final hole, and now he has to buy the round.

GOLF
ETIQUETTE
AND
SAFETY

17 ENJOY THE GAME

Jay Morelli, Director of the Original Golf School,
Mount Snow, Vermont

Golf is a most enjoyable game when played in four-and-a-half hours or less. Some things you can do to make sure your foursome keeps pace include:

1. Have the club in your hand before it is your turn to play the stroke.
2. Have the ball and tee in your hand when it is your turn to tee off.
3. Hit your ball within forty-five seconds of the previous player's stroke.
4. Suspend conversation and resume it after you have played your shot to avoid any unnecessary delay.
5. Play ready golf. Hit your shot as soon as it is safe to do so.

18 BUNKERS

Paul Glut, PGA Director of Golf, Woodside Acres Country Club, Syosset, New York

When playing a bunker shot, always enter the bunker from the low side, rather than stepping down the steep, high front of the bunker. After playing the shot, rake your divot and footprints. Place the rake parallel to the bunker and close to the edge. Knock the sand off your shoes so you do not leave sand footprints on the green.

19 ON THE GREEN

Mark Brown, PGA Director of Golf, Tam O'Shanter Club, Brookville, New York

When approaching the green, locate the balls to avoid walking through another player's line (the path the ball must travel from the lie to the hole). Repair any marks caused by the ball landing on the green. The player whose ball is closest to the pin should tend the pin. The first player to putt out should then pick up the pin and replace it after the last player putts out. Move to the next tee and record your score there, rather than on the edge of the green.

20 TEE TIMES
Paul Glut, PGA Director of Golf, Woodside Acres Country Club,
Syosset, New York

Many golfers make the mistake of getting to the course just prior to their tee times. When you cut it close, you run the risk of getting stuck in traffic or encountering other delays. Give yourself plenty of time to register, warm up, go to the putting green, and relax before you tee off. If you have a ten o'clock tee time, get to the course at nine. Check in with the starter twenty minutes before your assigned time. Allowing adequate time before you play greatly increases the chances that you will play well.

21 TAKE CARE OF THE COURSE
Karen Merritt, Golf Pro, North Salem, New York

A good golf course is a beautiful thing. Leave it in better shape than you found it. Repair ball markers. Replace divots. If the course provides sand, make sure to fill the divots. Do a good job raking bunkers after you've hit sand shots. A good question to ask yourself is this: "Would I be happy if I had to play from that spot?"

22 BE A GOOD PLAYING PARTNER
Scott Ford, PGA Teaching Pro, North Hills Country Club, Manhasset, New York

A few of the obvious rules are designed to show respect for your fellow players. When they are playing, stand still from the time they address the ball until the time the ball is on its way. Remember that the line of the putt is sacred. Never step in that line, as a small indentation in the green can throw the putt offline.

23 LOOK SHARP
Jay Morelli, Director of the Original Golf School, Mount Snow, Vermont

Golf is one of the few sports that doesn't require a uniform, so it's the perfect opportunity to look sharp. The best players, from Bobby Jones to Keegan Bradley, always look great. They dress well—in style and neatly pressed. None of these greats ever showed up with a ruffled or not-ready-for-prime-time look. Dressing well shows respect for the game and for your fellow players. We all don't play our best, but the one thing we can do is look good.

Matthew McPhillips, Head Professional, Stratton Mountain Country Club, Stratton, Vermont

24 THE GOLF CART
Jay Morelli, Director of the Original Golf School, Mount Snow, Vermont

Golf carts are a way of life. On many courses they are even required when you play. Try to keep them as inconspicuous as possible. Park them a reasonable distance away from the player and in a three o'clock to five o'clock position—the same place you would be standing if you were not in the cart. Be aware of soft turf or wet areas. Golf carts are fairly heavy and can cause damage to the course. When there are cart paths, use them. You can't wear out the asphalt. If there are no paths, try to "scatter." This spreads out the traffic and is easier on the turf.

25 GOLF CART RULES

Jay Morelli, Director of the Original Golf School, Mount Snow, Vermont

Here are some of the basic cart rules in the golf world:

1. Place your clubs behind where you plan to sit.
2. Observe cart rules. If it's "cart paths only," then all four tires should be on the cart path at all times.
3. When you leave the cart to play your stroke, take several clubs.
4. Never drive the cart within sixty feet (18 meters) of the green.
5. At the green, park the cart on the way to the next tee.
6. Write down the scores on the way to or on the next tee.
7. Don't park your cart on a hill.

26 TURN OFF YOUR CELL PHONE

Tom Herzog, PGA Teaching Pro, the Champions Course,
CedarBrook Country Club, Old Brookville, New York

There are a few people who need cell phone access all the time. They are doctors, other medical people, and those who deal with urgent issues. Most of us do not. If you are in that medical group, set the phone on "vibrate." If you are like me (and most of the rest of the world), leave the cell phone in the car. Cell phones ringing on the course not only disrupt you, but also those you are playing. If you must answer it or make a call, do it very quickly so no one even knows you made the call.

27 GOLF CART SAFETY

Jay Morelli, Director of the Original Golf School, Mount Snow, Vermont

While golf is not quite as dangerous as football or rugby, accidents do happen. As with all accidents, common sense must prevail at all times. While golf carts appear to be safe, there have been some weird and nasty accidents with them. A big problem is riding with your limbs hanging out of the golf cart. The most noticeable violators are players who ride with a foot outside the golf cart. If your foot is hanging out of the golf cart and there is any type of curb on the cart path, you stand a good chance of getting your foot caught between the golf cart and the curb. Ouch!

28 GOING UP?
Jay Morelli, Director of the Original Golf School, Mount Snow, Vermont

Another problem that occurs is driving the carts on slopes. The cart can tip over, especially when the grass is wet. This also tends to occur more often with the faster gas-powered carts. It's also important to drive straight up and down all slopes. There are no seat belts in golf carts, and it's very easy for a quick turn to toss a passenger out.

29 WHERE TO STAND
Greg Pace, PGA Teaching Pro, Huntington Country Club, Huntington, New York

Golf has its own culture. When your fellow players are hitting their shots, you should be still. Stand either completely behind them so they cannot see you or be to their side. To get the picture, if the line to the target is twelve o'clock and a line directly away is six o'clock, you should be at an angle that would be between 3:30 and 5:30. The absolute wrong place to stand is directly behind the line of flight or the line of the putt.

30 LOOKING FOR YOUR GOLF BALL

Mark Brown, PGA Director of Golf, Tam O'Shanter Club,
Brookville, New York

When we hit an offline shot, we often look up at the sky instead of marking a spot where the ball first went awry. Upon hitting the ball into a questionable location, first take note of its area as best you can from your location. Then take a maximum of two minutes to search for the ball after arriving in its general location. If the ball cannot be found within two minutes, drop a ball at the nearest point free of obstructions.

31 PRACTICE SWINGS

Jeff Seavey, PGA Teaching Pro, Samoset Resort Golf Club, Rockport, Maine

Practice swings should always be made toward the target or toward an open area with no other golfers nearby. In a practice swing, a player may hit the ground, which could turn up a stone, an old tee, or some other object. If you take a practice swing at another player, she might get hit by that object. Once in a great while, the head will fly off a club. A flying club head is a very dangerous weapon.

32 YELL "FOUR" AND BE ALERT WHEN YOU HEAR IT

John Gaeta, PGA Teaching Pro, North Hills Country Club, Manhasset, New York

Even if you follow the advice above, there will surely come times when you hit your driver farther than you expected, or a hook or slice comes out of nowhere and takes your ball toward an adjoining fairway. Or you may play your stroke believing the fairway is clear, only to notice players up ahead who had been obscured by a hill or tree.

33 DON'T THROW YOUR CLUBS

Jay Morelli, Director of the Original Golf School, Mount Snow, Vermont

I know this sounds like an absurd tip, but I've seen it happen. Golfers should never throw their clubs. If you have to throw a fit, go ahead, but you can cause real harm to someone with an airborne club.

34 KIDS

Jay Morelli, Director of the Original Golf School, Mount Snow, Vermont

One of my biggest concerns is when adults practice with small kids and even toddlers in the area. A swinging golf club is a dangerous weapon. Children have no idea where they should stand or what they should do, and the adults are often so involved in their practice that they forget the kids are underfoot. The kids should have a specific spot to sit or be and they should always be supervised by an adult other than the one who is practicing.

35 LATHER UP
Destiny Schaffer, Teaching Pro, Hilton Head, South Carolina

Keep sunscreen in your golf bag—even on those hazy, overcast days—and don't forget to use it. You'll be surprised at how much sun you'll get even when you think sun isn't an issue. Also, wear a wide-brimmed hat to shade your face.

36 LIGHTNING
John Gaeta, PGA Teaching Pro, North Hills Country Club, Manhasset, New York

We usually play golf in warm weather, when there are bound to be thunderstorms. They have to be respected. Many courses have meteorological warning systems, and while they are very good, they are not infallible. Come in at the first sign of an approaching storm, and if you are caught out in the storm, remember that you should stay away from metal and high ground. Seek shelter in a grounded rain shelter or a low-lying area.

CHAPTER 3

PRE-SHOT ROUTINE

37 PRE-SHOT ROUTINE FOR CONSISTENCY

Matthew McPhillips, PGA Head Golf Pro, Stratton Mountain Country Club, Stratton, Vermont

A pre-shot routine is the routine you perform before every shot. It should be consistent. As part of your pre-shot routine, always pick a target within several feet that is on a direct line to the ultimate target. Focus on a target a short distance away in order to aim the club face more accurately at address. It is also better to plan your aim while looking down the line to the target. Picking an intermediate target is sort of like spot bowling or picking a spot on the lane, rather than looking at the head pin.

38 PUTTING ROUTINE

Shawn Baker, PGA Director of Golf, the Greens at Half Hollow,
Melville, New York

A pre-shot routine is every bit as important when you putt as when you play a full shot. A good routine looks like this:

1. Determine your line.
2. Stand to the side of the ball, taking a few practice strokes while looking at the hole and trying to match your stroke to the distance.
3. Look down the line of the putt at the speed you expect the ball to roll (just like the "tracking" you see when watching the pros on TV). Do this three times.
4. Make a good stroke.

39 CORRECT MEASUREMENT FROM THE BALL

Dana Bates, LPGA Teaching Pro, Quaker Ridge Golf Club, Scarsdale, New York

When setting up to the golf ball, start by placing the bottom edge of your club flush to the ground. Then assume your stance. Adjust your stance as well as your posture with respect to the golf club and ball. Most golfers assume their stance first and then place the club head behind the ball. This results in the "toe" of the club being up, meaning the only part of the club face that can solidly hit the ball is the inside, or heel. We only have a couple of inches (5–7.5 centmeters) of club face to hit the ball with. Don't make it any smaller than it already is!

40 LOGICAL BALL POSITION

Dick Capasso, PGA Teaching Pro, Augusta, Georgia

Many players get confused about where to play the ball in their stance for shots off the turf. We have all heard conflicting advice on this subject. Each shot is a new experience and should be treated as such. The best place to place your ball is in the way of your swing. Try taking a few practice swings and pay attention to where the club nips the turf. That spot is where the ball should be played for that particular stroke.

41 TARGET AWARENESS

Jay Morelli, Director of the Original Golf School, Mount Snow, Vermont

One major way to improve is to be aware of the target. When we watch great players, we notice that they take great care in setting up to the ball. After they set up, we also see them look up at the target several times. It is part of their routine. They will always take the same number of looks. This is the same as a basketball player looking at the hoop at the free throw line. Most recreational golfers stare at the ball and get "ball bound," with little or no awareness of where they are trying to hit the ball. Try to build some looks into your pre-shot routine. It's a surefire way to move your game up a level.

42 TWO THOUGHTS

Barry Reynolds, PGA Teaching Pro, the Original Golf School, Mount Snow, Vermont

Start the season by promising yourself that you'll have only these two thoughts:

1. A pre-swing thought.
2. An in-swing thought.

   Bad golf shots will always be a result of too much analysis. We have often heard that we might get paralysis from analysis. Your pre-shot thought could be an idea about alignment, posture, or grip pressure. Your in-swing thought might focus on swing path, tempo, or a good shoulder turn. Keeping it simple is the goal.

43 FINDING THE CORRECT BALL POSITION

John Schob, PGA Director of Golf, the Huntington Crescent Club, Huntington, New York

Where the ball is positioned in your stance is crucial to solid contact. The best way to establish the center of your stance is to stand opposite the ball with your feet together. Take a small step to the left and a small step to the right and the ball will be dead center in your stance. You can change the ball position by taking a larger step in one direction than the other. For right-handed players, a small step with the left foot and a larger step with the right will position the ball left center in the stance, which is where you would like it with a driver.

44 DISTANCE TO THE BALL
Ron Johnson, PGA Teaching Pro, Somerset, New Jersey

How far away you stand from the ball at address is an important factor in making solid contact. To achieve the correct distance, hold the club waist-high, with your upper arms touching your chest. Tilt from the hips and stick out your tailbone, letting the club head sole rest on the ground. That is the correct distance. With a longer club, you will naturally be farther away than with a shorter one. Being the correct distance is the only way you can achieve proper balance. (If you tend to lose your balance and fall forward at the end of your swing, you are definitely standing too far from the ball.)

45 REMEDY FOR THE SHAKES
Shawn Baker, PGA Director of Golf, the Greens at Half Hollow, Melville, New York

You feel the panic setting in. Your hands get clammy, and your knees shake. Your throat goes dry, and you feel as if you're going to throw up. Golf is the ultimate pressure-situation sport, and it pays to remember the first (and only) rule for relaxing: Slow down and concentrate on your breathing. Take a few deep breaths as you prepare for that big shot.

THE LONG GAME

GOLF GRIP TERMS
Don Beatty, PGA Director of Golf, Garden City Country Club, Garden City, New York

We often hear golfers talk about a "strong" or "weak" grip. What are they talking about? The placement of the hands on the handle of the club. The placement of the hands affects every part of the golf swing and the distance the player will hit the ball. In a strong grip, a "V" formed by the thumb and forefingers of both hands will point below the back shoulder. In a weak grip, that "V" will point to your chin. In a neutral grip, that "V" will point to the back ear.

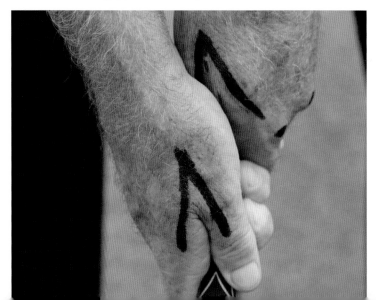

47 WHICH GRIP IS BEST FOR ME?
Don Beatty, PGA Director of Golf, Garden City Country Club,
Garden City, New York

A weak grip should be used only by very strong players who tend to hook the ball too much. A strong grip should be used by most players, as the player will easily be able to return the club face squarely to the ball. Many expert players use a strong grip. A neutral grip can be used by advanced players who have no problem slicing the ball.

48 THE VARDON GOLF GRIP
Shawn Baker, PGA Director of Golf, the Greens at Half Hollow,
Melville, New York

The Vardon Grip was introduced by the great English player, Harry Vardon. His concept was to somewhat join the hands so they would act more like one unit on the handle of the club. To use this grip, slip the pinky finger of your right hand over the space between the forefinger and middle finger of your left hand. The club is held in the palms and fingers of the left hand and more in the fingers of the right hand. This grip is recommended for players with medium to large hands.

Vardon grip

49 KEEP YOUR ELBOWS TOGETHER

Tom Joyce, PGA Pro Emeritus, Glen Oaks Golf Club, Maiden, North Carolina

One of my keys has always been to try to keep my elbows the same distance apart during the swing. If my elbows are four to five inches (10–12.5 centimeters) apart at address, they should be the same distance apart in the takeaway, the top of the backswing, at impact, and in the follow-through. The more the arms can stay that same distance apart, the more consistently I, and my students, will play.

50 CAN I USE THE INTERLOCKING GRIP?

Matthew Guyton, PGA Teaching Pro, Old Westbury Golf & Country Club, Old Westbury, New York

Several great players use the interlocking grip—Jack Nicklaus and Tiger Woods, to name two of the best. To use this grip, place the pinky of the right hand between the forefinger and middle finger of the left hand. The club is held in the palms and fingers of the left hand and more in the fingers of the right hand. This grip is recommended for players with small- to medium-size hands.

51 THE BASEBALL GRIP

Ron McDougal, PGA Director of Golf, Old Westbury Golf & Country Club, Old Westbury, New York

The ten-finger or "baseball" grip puts all your fingers on the club. You simply place the hands close to each other on the club, but they are not joined in any way. This is a good method for players who find the other two grips uncomfortable or who have small hands. Players should try different styles of holding the club, as it is very much a personal preference.

52 THE GOLF GRIP

Ron McDougal, PGA Director of Golf, Old Westbury Golf & Country Club, Old Westbury, New York

The most important part of the golf swing is the proper grip. The grip must be correct so the wrists hinge properly on the backswing and unhinge properly on the forward swing. This hinging is similar to the hinges on a door. As the club face swings on the backswing, the toe of the club appears to open. As the club face hits the ball, the club face will be square. After the ball has been struck, the club face will rotate and appear to close. Holding the handle of the club in the fingers and high in the palm in the top hand will ensure the proper grip and hinging.

53 THE HANDLE MUST LEAD THE CLUB HEAD

Scott Hawkins, PGA Director of Golf, Glen Head Country Club, Glen Head, New York

For solid contact with the golf ball, the handle of the club must be ahead of the club head at impact. Most golfers instinctively try to lift the ball into the air, allowing the club head to pass the ball. The result is a scooping action that is not powerful or consistent. In a good swing, the handle is ahead of the club face, and your body weight is on your front foot when you strike the ball.

54 THE CORRECT GRIP

John Cleanthes, PGA Teaching Pro, Haystack Golf Club, Wilmington, Vermont

Turn the top hand (the left for right-handed players) over a little. This is correct for all golfers and particularly good for players looking to correct a slice. When you take your grip, you should not be able to see the fingernails of your top hand. If the top hand is not over far enough, you will have trouble squaring the club face at impact.

55 GRIP PRESSURE

Jay Morelli, Director of the Original Golf School,
Mount Snow, Vermont

How tightly you hold on to the club can certainly affect the flight of the ball. Hooking, slicing, and straight shots can be created by different grip pressure. Soft grip pressure will promote a normal release and rotation of the club. The resulting shot will be a draw. Tighter grip pressure will reduce the amount of release and promote a straight shot or a slice. A very tight grip will restrict the release, which will produce a slice. At no time should the club be held very tightly.

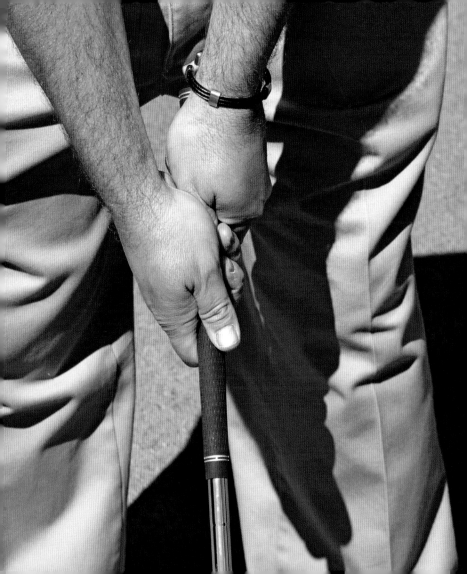

56 GRIP IT IN THE FINGERS
Mary Slinkard-Scott, PGA/LPGA Teaching Pro, the Plantation Golf Resort, Crystal River, Florida

Grip the handle of the golf club in the fingers for straighter and longer shots. Many golfers hold the handle in the palm of the top hand. This is a weak position and results in a slice and a lack of power. To get the proper feel of finger and palm, turn your club upside down so you are holding the shaft. Take your hand on and off the shaft a number of times until holding the club in your fingers begins to feel comfortable.

57 PERFECT POSTURE

Erik Sorensen, PGA Director of Golf, Dorset Field Club, Dorset, Vermont

The starting position in golf is crucial to establishing a strong, repeating swing. To attain the correct posture, stand straight, holding the club waist-high in front of you. Now tilt or bow from the hips. To balance the tilt, stick out your tailbone. Wherever the club touches the ground indicates the correct distance from the ball. Your spine should be straight but at an angle established by the tilt. (If you tilt from the hips and don't stick out your tailbone, your body weight will go to your toes and you will start the swing out of balance.) A good test is that you should be able to wiggle your toes in your shoes. That will show that your body weight is in the middle of your feet, where it should be.

58 YOUR KNEES AND YOUR GOLF SWING

Shawn Baker, PGA Director of Golf, the Greens at Half Hollow, Melville, New York

What happens to your knees while you're swinging the club will determine what type of shot you hit. Your back knee will straighten during your backswing (for some players, only a little; for others, a lot). Your front knee will bend on your backswing. What your knees do on the downswing will determine the contact you make with the ball and the ground, as well as what path your club will travel on the downswing. Here's how it breaks down:

1. The left knee should remain flexed. It has to move toward the target, eventually getting ahead of your left foot.
2. The right knee will regain the flex it had at address.
3. The left knee will begin to straighten on the downswing but remain slightly flexed until after impact. Then it will straighten.
4. The right knee will pivot toward the target.

59 THE CORRECT KNEE ACTION TO BETTER GOLF SHOTS

Douglas Miller, PGA Professional, Gold Coast Golf Center, Woodbury, New York

You can work on having the correct knee action to cure poor ball striking. Right-handed golfers who straighten the left leg and knee too soon will tend not to transfer their weight, creating an outside-to-inside swing, resulting in a high, weak slice. Strong players who tend to hook the ball too much would benefit from straightening the left leg sooner. Most average players would benefit from keeping the front knee bent as long as they possibly can in their swing.

A left-handed golfer working on his knee action.

60 THE BACK KNEE IS THE KEY

Douglas Miller, PGA Professional, Gold Coast Golf Center, Woodbury, New York

Some of the most common problems I see on the lesson tee include:

1. Topping the ball.
2. Failing to transfer weight to the forward foot.
3. Swaying during the swing.

The key is to focus on the right knee (the left knee for my left-handed friends). At the address position, both knees should be slightly flexed. Throughout the swing, think of the right knee and shin as a solid post—they will act as a stable base. This will make it much easier to move your left side during the downswing and will eliminate both the sway and the topped shot.

61 GOOD TEMPO

David Burnell, PGA Teaching Pro, Burlington Country Club, Burlington, Vermont

Good tempo is very important to great golf and low scores. There are keys to achieving the smoothest swing possible. Remember to relax *everything*—hands, arms, and shoulders. Breathe deeply. Stay in balance.

62 HIP, HIP, HOORAY!
Don Beatty, PGA Director of Golf, Garden City Country Club, Garden City, New York

Many errors in the golf swing are attributed to an incorrect rotation of the hips on the backswing. Many either sway the hips or don't allow them to turn at all. When you begin your backswing, allow your right hip (for right-handed players) to turn back. This will allow your shoulders to turn, which, in turn, will shift your weight to your back leg. At the top of your backswing, you should feel your weight on the inside of your back foot, and your back knee should be slightly bent. From this position, simply turn your right hip back into the shot.

63 SWING LIKE A SWAN

Amanda Arciero, PGA/LPGA Teaching Pro, Fresh Meadow
Country Club, Lake Success, New York

Years ago, I watched Ernie Els hit a 225-yard (206-meter) iron shot to the fifteenth green at the Masters. He swung so easily I thought he was laying up, yet the ball landed on the green! Ernie swings the club with effortless grace and style—a model for all of us. His rhythm and tempo on the backswing create stored power that is released at the bottom of his downswing. Most of us have the urge to start the backswing quickly, which will invariably make the start of the downswing fast. This quick start to the backswing and downswing will actually make the club head move more slowly through impact! Try to mimic the tempos of Ernie Els, Fred Couples, or Annika Sörenstam. They know how to swing like a swan, not a duck, and they look great!

Ernie Els (Photo courtesy of Bruce Curtis)

64 OBLIVIOUS TO THE OBVIOUS
Don Beatty, PGA Director of Golf, Garden City Country Club, Garden City, New York

All golfers should check their clubs for the wear patterns. Many golfers are unaware of where they are mis-hitting the ball. Look carefully at the faces of your clubs, particularly the short irons, to see where most of the contact is made. Off-center hits rob you of distance and accuracy. If you do see a wear pattern, simply do the opposite. If you tend to hit the ball off the toe of the club, address the ball in the heel. If you tend to hit the ball on the heel, address it on the toe. Golf is a game of opposites.

65 START THE SWING TOGETHER
Ron McDougal, PGA Director of Golf, Old Westbury Golf & Country Club, Old Westbury, New York

Years ago, I had the pleasure of playing with Tommy Bolt. He was one of the best ball strikers ever. I asked him what his key was in starting the swing. He said that everything simply went back together. Modern teachers would call this a *connected* swing. The club head, hands, arms, and center of the body stay together in the takeaway, and then throughout the swing.

66 BALANCE
Kevin Harrington, PGA Head Professional, Mount Snow Golf Club, West Dover, Vermont

If your drives aren't going well, remember that your balance is one of the biggest indicators of a proper swing. Good drivers of the ball finish standing tall, with weight on their forward foot, and with their belt buckle and the center of their body facing the target. If you can't hold this position until the ball hits the ground, you are out of balance. If you're having difficulty with your balance, try a balance rod. It will show you where your weight is distributed during your shot and quickly help you correct any imbalances.

67 WHAT DO YOU SWING AT?
Dick Capasso, PGA Teaching Pro, Augusta, Georgia

Most of my students say they swing at the ball. And most of them do. Good players swing at the target and just let the ball get in the way of the swing. Swinging at the ball creates a choppy swing with no follow-through. Swinging at the target creates a fluid swing with a full follow-through.

Using a balance rod.

68 ALIGNMENT

Ron McDougal, PGA Director of Golf, Old Westbury Golf & Country Club, Old Westbury, New York

To play well, you have to be aligned properly. The feet, hips, and shoulders are all aligned parallel to the line of flight. An experienced player can line all parts open, as Lee Trevino did. Sam Snead lined all parts closed. Most professional players today line feet, hips, and shoulders parallel to the target. It is very difficult to play if the feet are closed and the shoulders are open, or vice versa. It's like the transmission of a car. The gears must be lined up so all the parts work together smoothly.

69

THE TRANSITION

Tom Herzog, PGA Teaching Pro, the Champions Course, CedarBrook Country Club, Old Brookville, New York

At the top of the swing, the backswing is completed and we start the downswing. That transition from backswing to downswing must be smooth. The tendency is to make too hard a move from the top. This will ruin any chance of a powerful, repeatable swing. Soft grip pressure will also help you make that smooth transition.

70 IRON PLAY
Amanda Arciero, PGA/LPGA Teaching Pro, Fresh Meadow Country Club, Lake Success, New York

When hitting irons, your focus should be on having the leading edge of the club contact the bottom or base of the ball. Many players look at the whole ball or at the top of the ball, resulting in *topped,* or *thin,* shots. Focusing on having the leading edge of the club meet the bottom of the ball will help ensure solid contact.

71 LESS IS MORE
Dick Capasso, PGA Teaching Pro, Augusta, Georgia

We all know that feeling of the "easy" hit, when a smooth swing produces our best shot. One key to those shots is the smooth, unforced backswing. Remember that "less is more" on the backswing. You can't hit it on the backswing, so a smooth backswing will give you more control as you ease into the downswing. It will also set you up to make a strong, effective, and powerful downswing.

Iron play

72 TRUST THE LOFT

Paul Glut, PGA Director of Golf, Woodside Acres Country Club, Syosset, New York

We often use the driver to try to "help" get the ball in the air. The most effective way to hit with the driver is to swing the club head low on the backswing. This should help create a shallow path on the downswing. If you do that, the loft of the driver will get the ball airborne. It's a matter of trusting the loft of the club.

73 POSITION OF THE RIGHT LEG AND FOOT

Shawn Baker, PGA Director of Golf, the Greens at Half Hollow, Melville, New York

When Ben Hogan won the British Open at Carnoustie in 1953, he told his caddie he played well because his right knee never moves. The position of the right leg and knee (for right-handers) is crucial to good shots. The right foot should be perpendicular to the line of flight. The right knee should be flexed and pointed slightly inward. In the perfect swing, the body will wind up and actually coil around the right knee. It should stay flexed and stable throughout the swing. In the follow-through, the right foot is released and you finish on the right toe.

74 RELAX FOR BETTER GOLF
Jay Morelli, Director of the Original Golf School,
Mount Snow, Vermont

It is important to relax when you address the golf ball. The correct grip and posture are the keys to good golf, and they can only be attained by first relaxing. Players tend to get a death grip on the club. It's just human nature. The best way to relax is to start by holding the handle of the club softly. Staying relaxed and soft in the grip is the only way you can be in position to make a smooth swing at the target. After you have established a good, relaxed grip and posture, focus on the target and make a good swing.

75 HITTING THE BALL ON THE DOWNBEAT

Shawn Baker, PGA Director of Golf, the Greens at Half Hollow, Melville, New York

To be a good iron player, particularly with the short irons, you must hit the ball on the *downbeat*. The club face should solidly hit the ball and then take a long, shallow divot. This can only be done properly if the handle is ahead of the club face at contact. Most players try to scoop the ball into the air, letting the club head get ahead of the handle. This error will result in hitting behind or topping the ball. A good weight transfer and a good finish position will keep the handle in front of the club head and ensure solid contact.

76 HOW TO PLAY THE HYBRID

Joe Rehor, PGA Director of Golf, Bethpage State Park,
Farmingdale, New York

The widespread use of hybrid clubs has certainly made a difference in the game. A good question is this: Should I play them like an iron or like a metal wood? For best results, play the hybrid as you would an iron. The ball should be just about dead center in the stance. While you do not take a divot with the hybrid, you should at least brush the grass when you swing to make sure the middle of the club gets down to the middle of the ball. Also, for best results, do not position the ball forward with the hybrid as you would with a metal wood, but position it in the middle of your stance.

Hybrid club

77 IT'S HIP TO BE SQUARE

Jeff Pratt, PGA Teaching Pro, Tam O'Shanter Club, Brookville, New York

Here's a little exercise to help you set up properly. Go to the kitchen with golf club in hand and set up on your tile floor. (You, of course, can also do this exercise on the golf course.) Place your feet on one parallel line, put the club face perpendicular to a target line that is parallel to your stance, and now you are officially square. Being square gives you a better chance of hitting the ball solidly and straight with your feet in the correct position, and your shoulders, arms, hips, and club face square to the target. Now the fun begins!

78 HOLD THE FINISH
*Amanda Arciero, PGA/LPGA Teaching Pro, Fresh Meadow
Country Club, Lake Success, New York*

If your balance is good at address and throughout the swing, you will be able to hold your finish at the end of the swing. We all know that balance is the real key to consistent golf. Try to hold your finish after every shot. If you're having trouble maintaining your balance, check your starting position and the distance you stand from the ball. You must start in good balance to be able to finish in balance.

79 SWING A BASKETBALL

Michael T. Wanser, PGA Teaching Pro, Cherry Valley Club, Garden City, New York

Connection between the arms and the body is a very important aspect in a repetitive, efficient golf swing. Swinging a basketball is a great way to feel the proper connection and sequence

during a golf swing motion. Assume your golf posture and hold a basketball. Swing the ball away, using your arms and body together as you make your backswing. Having the ball in your hands establishes the connection between your arms and your body. Then simply imagine throwing the ball down the fairway as you swing through. This action will provide the correct sequence of motion, with your lower body leading the way.

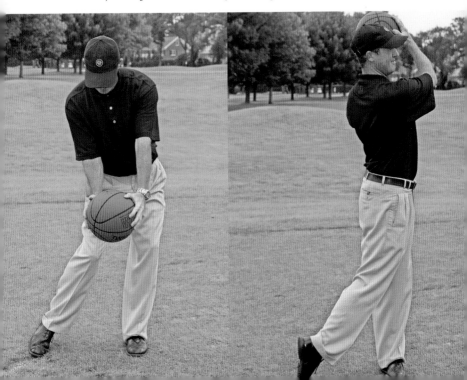

80 LAUNCH ANGLE

*Matthew Guyton, PGA
Teaching Pro, Old Westbury
Golf & Country Club, Old
Westbury, New York*

To maximize your distance with the driver, you should have the correct "launch angle" as the ball leaves the face of the driver. This launch angle will vary from player to player, depending on strength and club head speed. This angle is determined by a launch monitor, which is best used by a trained professional. It is worth the investment in time and money to find the driver that fits you best.

CHAPTER 5

CHIP AND PITCH SHOTS

81 THE CHIP SHOT

Jay Morelli, Director of the Original Golf School, Mount Snow, Vermont

The chip-and-run shot is a real stroke saver. Visualize the chip, where will it land, and how far it will run. To play it, position the ball slightly back in the stance. Your hands will then be slightly ahead of the club head, creating an angle. Try to maintain that angle throughout the chip stroke. Your weight should be a little on your forward foot. This setup will create a slightly descending club head angle. Swing through smoothly and hold the angle to a low finish.

82 IDENTIFY THE LIE
Tom Joyce, PGA Pro Emeritus, Glen Oaks Golf Club, Maiden, North Carolina

Before you overthink the mechanics of any shot, you have to identify the lie. Is the ball sitting up in the grass or is it in a little depression? The ball will react differently depending on the lie. If the ball is sitting up, with some grass underneath, it will go higher and softer off the club face. If the ball is sitting down, it will come out of the lie lower and faster. Recognizing how the ball will react is not something you try to change; rather, it's something you adjust for.

83 CONTROL THE DISTANCE OF THE CHIP SHOT

Tom Joyce, PGA Pro Emeritus, Glen Oaks Golf Club, Maiden, North Carolina

Chipping is simply putting with a medium-lofted club, like a 5 to 8 iron. The length and the pace of the swing control distance. The backswing and follow-through should be the same. The swing should be in rhythm. On a short chip, there should be a short backswing and follow-through. On a longer chip, both the backswing and follow-through should be longer and equal in length. Just as in putting, it's good to make the swing similar to the motion of a pendulum.

84 DON'T SCOOP THE CHIP SHOT

Andy Hardiman, PGA Teaching Pro, Quaker Ridge Golf Club, Scarsdale, New York

Most golfers try to scoop the ball up when they chip, resulting in either hitting behind the ball or topping it. To prevent this, I suggest using a putting grip, even on chip shots. Extend the left forefinger down the shaft, and then make your normal putting stroke. Change clubs for desired distance and action. Use a fairly straight-faced club, like a 6 or 7 iron, on long chips where you have a lot of green to run the ball. Use a more lofted club, like an 8 or 9 iron, when you do not have a lot of green to work with. This helps eliminate the pressure involved in the shot, and you will gain more confidence.

85 CRISP CHIP SHOTS
Marc Turnesa, PGA Director of Golf, Rockville Links Club,
Rockville Centre, New York

The setup is very important in order to hit a chip shot crisply.
Your weight should be slightly forward, so you are leaning a little
toward the target. Ball position should be center or slightly back
in the stance. The handle of the club must stay forward of the
club head through contact. Hit the ball with a descending blow,
taking a small divot after the shot.

86 THE SIZE OF YOUR SWING
Wendy Modic, LPGA Teaching Pro, Fenway Golf Club, Scarsdale,
New York

You should vary the size of your swing with the distance of the
chip or pitch shot. To get a good picture of this, imagine yourself
standing in the face of a clock, with the ball and your feet at the
six o'clock position and your head at the twelve o'clock position.
Swing the club from five o'clock to seven o'clock for the shortest
shots, four o'clock to eight o'clock for a longer shot, and three
o'clock to nine o'clock for still longer shots.

Practice varying the size of your swing.

87 FLIP, FLOP, AND FLUB NO MORE!

Tom Joyce, PGA Pro Emeritus, Glen Oaks Golf Club, Maiden, North Carolina

The number-one most common error in chipping is when the club head passes the hands before impact. This produces the dreaded flip, flop, or flub. Uncocking of the wrists before impact creates a scooping impact that will never lead to consistency. On your downswing, your hands must lead the way down, delaying the release of the club head until the last possible moment. The shaft of the club will be leaning slightly toward the target, which will create crisp and solid shots. Impact errors during chip shots are often attributed to an incorrect address position. At address, make sure you:

1. Set your hands slightly ahead.
2. Lean a little toward the target.
3. Narrow your stance.
4. Position the ball slightly back of center.

Practice these simple fundamentals and you will be a former flipper, flopper, and flubber!

88 CALIBRATE YOUR SHORT SHOTS

Don Beatty, PGA Director of Golf, Garden City Country Club, Garden City, New York

Around the green we need very short swings for short shots and slightly longer swings for longer shots. To calibrate these different-size swings, try to place your feet together, get close to the ball, and shorten way up on the handle for very short shots. As the shots around the green get longer, stand a little farther from the ball, slightly widen your stance, and don't shorten up on the handle quite as much. Shortening up on the handle and getting closer to the ball will help you think small, so you won't make too big a swing.

89 DON'T FINESSE THE SHOT

John Meckstroth, PGA Teaching Pro, the Original Golf School, Mount Snow, Vermont

If there has ever been a thought that has wrecked golf scores, it's the idea of *finessing* the ball to the target. Even short shots must be hit decisively. Rather than finessing the shot, think of hitting the ball solidly with a shorter swing.

90 GRIP PRESSURE ON CHIP SHOTS

Guna Kunjan, PGA Director of Golf, Harbor Links Golf Course,
Port Washington, New York

Grip pressure depends on how the ball is sitting in the grass. If the ball is sitting up, grip pressure should be soft, and you should use a smooth and sweeping motion. If the ball is sitting down in the grass, you should hold the handle more firmly. A firmer grip will produce a little more downward pressure, which will loft the ball from the turf.

91 CHIPPING TO VERY FAST GREENS

Barry Reynolds, PGA Teaching Pro, the Original Golf School, Mount Snow, Vermont

When the greens are like lightning, you should soften the chip shots so they don't run too much. To do this:

1. Shorten up on the handle so your hands are at the bottom of the grip.
2. Stand very close to the ball so the heel of the club face comes off the ground.
3. Weaken your grip (for right-handed players this means turning your left hand to the left) and soften your grip pressure.
   This will guarantee soft, spinning shots.

92 CHIP LIKE YOU PUTT

Mary Slinkard-Scott, PGA/LPGA Teaching Pro, Plantation Golf Resort, Crystal River, Florida

You should address the chip as you would address a putt, with eyes over the ball. This will affect how the club sits on the ground. Rather than soling the club so it is flat on the ground, it will rest somewhat on the toe of the club. Next, just make a good putting stroke with the chipping club.

93 DOWN IS UP, UP IS DOWN

Joe Rehor, PGA Director of Golf, Bethpage State Park,
Farmingdale, New York

A good phrase to remember when playing short shots is this: "Down is up and up is down." To hit the ball in the air, you have to hit it on the downbeat and brush the grass. If you try to lift the ball up with the club head, the ball will stay on the ground. You can't lift the ball. Any lifting lifts the club off the grass, creating a "topped" shot.

94 BRUSH THE GRASS

*Tom Joyce, PGA, Pro
Emeritus, Glen Oaks
Golf Club, Maiden,
North Carolina*

A simple technique to help you get the feel for the chip shot is to brush the grass during the practice swing. This brushing action is the best possible chipping stroke because the club head stays low to the ground, making solid contact a given.

95 THE BLADED WEDGE
Josh Shepard, PGA Director of Golf, Muttontown Club, East Norwich, New York

The ball sometimes comes to rest just off the green, on the apron and against a cut of rough. This is a difficult shot because if you try to chip the ball you will snag the grass behind the ball. The way to play this shot is to use the shortest wedge in your bag, either the sand or the lob wedge. Open the stance and open the club face. Use a putting stroke. Make sure the leading edge of the wedge contacts the equator of the ball. The ball will roll like a putt.

96 CHIPPING WITH A HYBRID

Joe Rehor, PGA Director of Golf, Bethpage State Park,
Farmingdale, New York

Many players chip and pitch the ball with the hybrid. The hybrid is very reliable and will produce a running shot. To play the hybrid to chip with:

1. Use the shortest hybrid in your bag.
2. Shorten up on the handle to make the hybrid feel as if it's the same length as the putter.
3. Use a long putting-style stroke.

It takes some practice to get a feel for how much swing to use for the distance. (This is a great idea for players who have been chronically poor chippers.)

97 CHANGE CLUBS TO SUIT THE CONDITIONS

Joe Rehor, PGA Director of Golf, Bethpage State Park, Farmingdale, New York

Conditions on the course change constantly. It's best to choose the correct loft for the situation. When chipping into a strong wind, take a less lofted club, such as the 6 iron, instead of the 7 iron. The ball will stay lower and will reach the hole. On the other hand, if you're chipping with a strong wind behind you, choose the 8 iron instead of the 7. This will make it less likely that the ball will go sailing past the hole. Trust your gut to help you adjust to the ever-changing conditions.

98 CHIPPING AND PITCHING

John Meckstroth, PGA Teaching Pro, the Original Golf School, Mount Snow, Vermont

On both chip and pitch shots, all you are trying to do is hit the ball solidly. To do this, position the ball back in the stance and keep more weight on the forward foot. This will ensure that the ball is hit with a descending swing. It's important to let the club swing toward the target, not to steer or overcontrol the club head.

99 KEEP YOUR ARMS MOVING
Marc Turnesa, PGA Director of Golf, Rockville Links Club,
Rockville Centre, New York

A good and simple key for all shots around the green is to keep your arms moving. Most missed hits occur when the player quits on the swing. So keeping your arms moving will get you through the ball and help you attain the necessary follow-through.

100 THE PITCH SHOT
Melissa Rath, Teaches Clinics, CedarBrook Golf Club,
Old Brookville, New York

The first step when you approach a pitch shot is to assess the lie. Place the club head behind the ball to see if you can slide the club head through the grass and below the ball. If the ball is too tight to the ground, a different kind of shot is needed. If the lie is good, position the ball slightly forward of center in your stance. Your weight should be slightly forward, with 60 percent on your forward foot. Visualize your shot. I like to think my swing is similar to a roller coaster—a slow ascent, a slight hesitation, and then an acceleration down and through.

101 THE PITCH SHOT, REDUX

Matthew Guyton, PGA Teaching Pro, Old Westbury Golf & Country Club, Old Westbury, New York

The pitch shot is the shot you make from about five to fifty yards (5–50 meters). It is usually played with a wedge. To play this shot, your stance and your club head should be square. The ball should be in the center of your stance. Your hands are about even with the club head. To be consistent, feel your arms lying softly on your body at address. Your arms should move with your body and stay connected to your body throughout the swing. Hold the finish to ensure a full, balanced follow-through.

102 LISTEN FOR A GOOD PITCH SHOT

Marc Turnesa, PGA Director of Golf, Rockville Links Club, Rockville Centre, New York

A good way to improve your pitch shot is to listen to the sound the club makes during the practice swing. When the club is swung properly, it will just graze the top of the grass, making a swishing sound. If the club is swung improperly, the club head will dig into the ground, creating a dull thud. This is a fun way to create the correct pitch swing.

103 HEAVY GRASS
Barry Reynolds, PGA Teaching Pro, the Original Golf School, Mount Snow, Vermont

Heavy grass around the greens makes golfing difficult. Try my method (which I learned on the Champions Tour). Select a sand wedge. Address the ball well back in the stance, opposite your back foot. Loosen your grip considerably. Move your hands forward so they are over your left knee (for right-handed players) and then swing the club. This may seem confusing. It is worth rereading. The ball will pop out of the lie and run quite a bit. A little practice and experience will go a long way on this shot.

104 PITCH SHOTS ON THE DOWNBEAT

Jason Lyons, PGA Teaching Pro, Rockville Links Club, Rockville Centre, New York

The single most important concept in the pitch shot is to hit it on the downswing. The club head must be descending if the ball is going to achieve proper trajectory and loft. The feeling in the pitch shot is that you're going to press the ball against the turf. When you contact the ball, your hands should be ahead of the club head. The downward action and loft of the club will lift the ball into the air.

105 THE FLOP SHOT

Clifford Bouchard, PGA Teaching Pro, Haystack Golf Club, Wilmington, Vermont

This is a high, short shot, used to go over a bunker or hit to an elevated green. The best clubs for this are the sand wedge and the lob wedge. You need a fairly good lie if this is going to be played well. Play the ball forward in your stance; open your stance; make a big, slow swing; and keep your arms moving. You should finish the swing facing the target with your weight on your forward foot. The ball will fly nice and high, and land softly with little or no roll.

SAND PLAY

106 THE GREENSIDE BUNKER SHOT

Fred Auletta, PGA Teaching Pro, Manchester Country Club, Bedford, New Hampshire

The greenside bunker shot is unique. It requires a slightly open stance, no weight shift, and an acutely descending swing plane, which causes the ball to rise quickly. The club face does not actually hit the ball, but enters the sand about two inches (5 centimeters) behind the ball. This stroke requires a full follow-through without letting the right hand cross over the left (for right-handed golfers). The size of the swing should match the distance of the shot.

107 MORE ON THE GREENSIDE BUNKER SHOT

Melissa Rath, Teaches Clinics, CedarBrook Club,
Old Brookville, New York

Bunker shots are the easiest shots in golf, as we do not even hit the ball. Practice by drawing a line in the sand in the center of your stance. This is the point where the club head will enter the sand, the same as a wedge shot off the grass. Take several practice swings with the club entering the sand as close to the sand as possible. When playing the shot, draw the line again and place the ball one and a half inches (3.8 centimeters) in front of the line. The club will enter the sand at the line, sliding under the ball and lofting the ball onto the green.

108 THE LONG GREENSIDE BUNKER SHOT (FOR ADVANCED PLAYERS)

Joe Elliott, PGA Teaching Pro, Garden City Country Club, Garden City, New York

The long bunker shot (more than seventy yards) using the normal bunker technique is difficult for even a strong player. The concept is to have the club head enter the sand about two inches (5 centimeters) behind the ball. The trick to getting enough distance is for the sand wedge to stay shallow throughout the swing. If the club head digs at all, you will never be able to get enough power. In order to ensure a strong, shallow swing, make the following change in your stance: After you have taken your stance, move back about an inch or two. This slight adjustment will keep the club head shallow, making it lot easier to move the sand and ball out of the bunker.

THE LONG GREENSIDE BUNKER SHOT, REDUX (FOR ADVANCED PLAYERS)

Matthew McPhillips, PGA Teaching Pro, Stratton Mountain Country Club, Stratton, Vermont

The long, greenside bunker shot, maybe thirty yards (27 meters), is one of the toughest shots in the game. It's hard to hit a

greenside bunker shot more than sixty-five feet (20 meters) without getting dangerously close to the ball. Use the same technique you would with a medium-length bunker shot, but use a 9 iron. Open the stance, lay the club back, hit an inch and a half behind the ball, and follow through. The less-lofted 9 iron will hit the ball farther. Practice with the 7 iron up to the pitching wedge to get a feel for how much distance each club will produce.

110 TEMPO IN THE SAND

Erik Sorensen, PGA Director of Golf, Dorset Field Club, Dorset, Vermont

The bunkers tend to get the best of the average player. As we get in the sand, we get anxious and usually swing hard and fast, resulting in a poor shot. We try to get the shot over too quickly. An often-overlooked aspect of good bunker play is good rhythm. Try to match the speed of the backswing with the speed of the downswing. A slower tempo will produce higher and softer shots. A hurried swing will create a steep swing and some digging. Keep the swing even and smooth for good bunker play.

111 THE CORRECT CLUB IN THE SAND

Clifford Bouchard, PGA Teaching Pro, Haystoack Golf Club, Wilmington, Vermont

Playing out of wet or firm sand can be very tricky. If you attempt to play these strokes with a 60-degree wedge with a wide flange, there is an excellent chance the club head will bounce off the sand and you will end up with a skulled shot or you will dig the club down too much into the sand. I suggest playing this shot with a thinner-soled, 56-degree wedge. This thinner-soled wedge will allow you to take the necessary divot of sand out of the bunker and will greatly reduce your chance of a thin or skulled shot. In general, if the sand is soft, you should use a sand wedge with a wide flange and a lot of bounce. If the bunkers are firm, you should use a sand wedge with a thin flange and minimal bounce.

112 THE BURIED BALL OR "FRIED EGG" IN THE BUNKER

Andrew Pohalski, Nassau Community College

So often we find the ball sitting in a footprint or hole in the bunker. When the ball is depressed, usually we are as well. To play this difficult shot, position the ball off your back toe. Your hands remain in the middle of your body. This will make the club face appear closed or hooded. The back ball position will create a steep downswing. Swing the head of the sand wedge down directly behind the ball. The loft of the sand wedge and the downward pressure of the swing will pop the ball up and out of the bunker. This shot often goes astray. That's something you just have to plan for.

113 THE DOWNHILL LIE IN A GREENSIDE BUNKER

Clifford Bouchard, PGA Teaching Pro, Haystack Golf Club, Wilmington, Vermont

This is a very difficult shot. If you play it as a normal bunker shot, you will most likely bounce the leading edge of the sand wedge into the ball and skull it over the green. Take a square, not open, stance. Play the ball back-center in the stance. (The club face will appear hooded or closed.) Swing the club head down and through. The sand wedge should enter the sand about one and a half inches (3.8 centimeters) behind the ball. The club head should swing down the hill, following the contour of the hill. The ball will come out of the lie fairly low, which you'll just have to plan for.

114 BALL RESTING NEAR THE FRONT EDGE OF THE BUNKER

Andrew Pohalski, PGA Director of Golf, Nassau Country Club, Glen Cove, New York

With this challenge most players have a tendency to try to lift the ball over the front lip of the bunker. To play this shot, open your stance, lay the face of your sand wedge back, and swing your club head into the hill, hitting about an inch (2.5 centimeters) behind the ball. The loft of the sand wedge and the force of the club head going down into the sand will lift the ball out of the bunker. The ball will normally come out high and soft from this lie.

115 THE SIDEHILL BUNKER SHOT WITH THE BALL ABOVE YOUR FEET (FOR ADVANCED PLAYERS)

Andrew Pohalski, PGA Director of Golf, Nassau Country Club, Glen Cove, New York

This is a difficult shot, since the sidehill will tend to make the sand wedge dig into the sand. The first step is to shorten up on the handle of the club. This will compensate for the ball being higher than usual. As with a regular sand shot, try to have the sand wedge enter the sand about one and a half inches behind the ball. The sand divot should not be deep. Keep your arms moving. The ball will usually "pull" on this shot and run more than normal.

116 NOSE OVER THE BALL

Andrew Pohalski, PGA Director of Golf, Nassau Country Club, Glen Cove, New York

A poor sand shot can add tons of strokes to your score. Most sand shots are missed because the player anticipates the results before the swing is completed. Coming out of the shot early normally results in catching the ball on the bottom of the club and having the ball sail over the green. Try keeping your nose over the ball in a sand shot. That will keep you steady and make sure you hit the sand behind the ball, as you should.

117 KEEP YOUR ELBOWS SLIGHTLY FLEXED

Andrew Pohalski, PGA Director of Golf, Nassau Country Club, Glen Cove, New York

Everyone who has ever played golf has hit a sand shot on the bottom of the club and watched the ball sail over the green. A good way to avoid this shot (and vanquish this fear) is to keep your elbows slightly flexed when you address the ball in the bunker. The force of your swing will automatically extend your arms. This extension will ensure that you hit the sand behind the ball.

118 IDENTIFY THE LIE IN THE BUNKER

Andrew Pohalski, PGA Director of Golf, Nassau Country Club, Glen Cove, New York

So much of golf is identifying how the ball sits in the bunker. If the ball is lying cleanly, you play the ball forward, hit behind it, and follow through. If the ball is in a hole, play it back, and bury the club head behind the ball. Take a good look at how the ball is sitting in the sand. If it's down even a little bit, play it as a buried lie. The worst that will happen is that the ball will come out, but be short of the hole. If you play a ball that is even slightly buried as a clean lie, there is a very good chance you will skull it and send it sailing across the green.

119 SAND TEXTURE

Andrew Pohalski, PGA Director of Golf, Nassau Country Club, Glen Cove, New York

The sand in bunkers can vary from course to course and locale to locale. The concepts in playing bunker shots won't vary, but the texture of the sand often will. A simple rule is this: The softer the sand, the more softly the ball will come out of the sand. The firmer the sand, the faster the ball will come out of the bunker. In soft sand, you have to swing harder. In firm sand, you'll need a less powerful swing.

120 THE TEXAS WEDGE OUT OF THE BUNKER

Andrew Pohalski, PGA Director of Golf, Nassau Country Club, Glen Cove, New York

Every now and then the ball will be in a flat bunker with no lip or edge. This is a great time to putt the ball out of the bunker. (The putter is often referred to as the Texas Wedge when used off the green.) The key to this is being able to visualize the shot. If there is any lip or edge, the ball will just hit the lip and stay in the bunker. This shot is easiest when the sand is firm and you don't have too much of the bunker to putt through.

121

A BALL UP AGAINST THE LIP OF THE BUNKER

Andrew Pohalski, PGA Director of Golf, Nassau Country Club, Glen Cove, New York

If you find your ball on the upslope of a bunker, under the lip, with a long distance to the flagstick, try using a less-lofted club than a sand wedge. An 8 iron will still give you enough loft to carry the lip and will produce enough forward momentum to reach that flagstick on the other side of the green. The ball position should be center, and your shoulders should be at the same angle as the slope of the bunker. Your weight will be on your back foot. Try to have the club head enter the sand two inches (5 centimeters) behind the ball. Open the face of the iron slightly so you achieve some bounce—this way the club head will not dig into the sand.

122 THE IMPOSSIBLE BUNKER SHOT

Michael T. Wanser, PGA Teaching Pro, Cherry Valley Club, Garden City, New York

A deep bunker with a huge lip in front may make it impossible to hit the ball at the green. If you think the shot to the green is impossible, it probably is. There are times when the correct bunker shot selection is to play the ball out to the side of the bunker. If you choose to play out safely to the side, make sure you are hitting the ball to a good level spot. If you hit the ball to an easy spot, you may be able to chip the ball close to the hole for a one putt. The important point is that you have played a smart shot that averted a very bad score.

PUTTING

123 THE PUTTING STROKE

Guna Kunjan, PGA Director of Golf, Harbor Links Golf Course, Port Washington, New York

The player should hold the handle of the putter more in the palms than in the fingers. Stand comfortably over the ball so that your eyes are directly over the ball. It's okay if your eyes are inside the line, but your eyes should never be outside the line. The putting stroke is initiated by the shoulders, not the hands. You should feel a rocking motion in the shoulders as you make the putting stroke. Hold the follow-through until the ball either goes in the hole or stops rolling. This will ensure an accelerating stroke.

124 THE PUTTING GRIP: THE REVERSE OVERLAP

Jay Morelli, Director of Golf, the Original Golf School, Mount Snow, Vermont

While there are many ways to hold a putter, one popular grip is called the *reverse overlap* grip. Take the forefinger of the top hand and overlap all the fingers of the bottom hand. This style marries the hands together. It also stretches the wrist on the top hand, making it easier to use more of an arm-and-shoulder putting stroke.

125 SOME PUTTING TIPS

Fred Auletta, PGA Teaching Pro, Manchester Country Club, Bedford, New Hampshire

To help get the feel of putting, try to open your right palm (for right-handed players) and swing your arm so the palm faces the hole. Get a feel for how much arm swing you need to achieve the required distance. You can feel as if the right palm is moving right to the hole. Try opening your stance a little so you can feel the right palm swinging toward the hole. The left elbow should be pointed toward the hole. The right arm should straighten on the follow-through. Don't just tap or try to hit the ball; instead, the head of the putter should follow through all the way to the hole.

126 MORE PUTTING TIPS

Kate Baker, LPGA Teaching Pro, Pebble Beach, California,
and the Greens at Half Hollow, Melville, New York

We all know how important putting is! Here are the steps I suggest:

1. Start behind the ball to determine the line of the putt.
2. Pick out an intermediate spot somewhere on that line and use that as a guide. You can also use the lettering on the ball as a line to the hole.
3. Visualize the putt.
4. Your arms should be relaxed and beside your body.
5. The most important step now is to commit to the line and trust that you have correctly read and lined up the putt. Most putts are missed by not committing and not trusting your putting stroke.

127 BALL POSITION AND THE DOMINANT EYE

Jay Morelli, Director of the Original Golf School,
Mount Snow, Vermont

To hit the putt solidly and be able to see the line, you have to determine your dominant eye. The dominant eye is the one responsible for sighting. To do this, point at a ball with your index finger. Look at the ball with both eyes. Then close one eye. Open it and then close the other. With one eye, the ball will stay in the same place (this is your dominant eye), while with the other, it will appear to move. The dominant eye is the one you sight the line with. If your left eye (for right-handed players) is your dominant eye, the ball should be played more forward in your stance. If your right eye is dominant, then the ball should be positioned more in the center of your stance. The best example of this is Jack Nicklaus. His eyes were over the line but behind the ball. He was a left-eye-dominant player.

128 USE A PLUMB BOB TO DETERMINE THE BREAK

Guna Kunjan, PGA Director of Golf, Harbor Links Golf Course, Port Washington, New York

We've all seen players stand behind a putt and hold the putter up, looking at the ball. They are determining the way the ball will curve or *break* on the green. Here's how it works:

1. Hold the putter at the end of the handle, high in the air.

2. With your dominant eye (close the other eye), line up the shaft, the ball, and the hole, so you can only see the shaft.

3. Now open your other eye. Give your eyes a chance to refocus.

4. If you've done this properly, the shaft will appear to move very slightly. The side it moves to is the high side of the hole. The amount it moves will not tell you how much it breaks.

This doesn't work for all golfers, but if it works for you, it will work every time.

129 READING THE BREAK
Guna Kunjan, PGA Director of Golf, Harbor Links Golf Course, Port Washington, New York

Determining which direction the ball will break takes experience. We see tournament players getting low to the ground to try to picture which way and how much the ball will break. This takes some imagination and visualization. It might be helpful to picture which way the water would flow if it were raining. Water obviously will flow downhill and the ball will bend the same way.

130 READING THE PUTT FROM THE LOW SIDE
Barry Reynolds, PGA Teaching Pro, the Original Golf School, Mount Snow, Vermont

The best side to look at a putt is from the low side, or the bottom of the slope of the green. When you are looking at the putt from the low side you are looking into the hill, giving you a much better feel for the terrain. It's like being at the bottom of a ski slope, looking up at the mountain. You can see everything. If you're at the top of that mountain, looking down, all the features are falling away from you and are harder to distinguish.

Reading the break.

131 MAKE EVERY PUTT A STRAIGHT PUTT

Kevin Harrington, Head Professional, Mount Snow Golf Club, West Dover, Vermont

Golfers may become confused with putts that have some break. After you read the putt and determine how much the slope will affect the line of the putt, think of the putt as a straight putt. If the putt will break six inches (15 centimeters), aim the lines or writing on the ball to that point. Putt the ball directly at that point and let the break take over. You can only start the ball on its course. Gravity does the rest.

132 THE RHYTHM OF THE PUTTING STROKE

Joe Cioe, Tournament Professional, PGA Tour

To control the distance you need when putting, you have to control the length of the stroke back and the stroke toward the hole. The backswing and forward stroke should be equal in length and in rhythm. Think of a pendulum. When the pendulum changes direction, it is unhurried. The ball should be in the middle of that pendulum swing. A smooth stroke will produce a pure roll.

133 WATCH THE BEST

Kevin Harrington, PGA Head Professional, Mount Snow Golf Club, West Dover, Vermont

All you have to do to improve your putting is watch how the great players putt. They all have soft grip pressure. None of them move their legs or hips. They each keep their head steady. They don't use any wrist break. They accelerate through the ball. If anything, their putting strokes are either the same size back as through, or their follow-through is longer than their back swing. They all hold their follow-through. Only the neck rotates after impact.

134 WALKING OFF THE PUTT

*Ann Obermeyer, LPGA Teaching Pro, the Village Club of
Sands Point, Sands Point, New York*

It's always a good idea to count the steps from your ball to the
hole. This doesn't take extra time. You can do it as you walk to the
ball. Every step is about two to three feet (.6 to 1 meter). (Take
the time to figure out your average step length.) So, if it's ten
steps from the hole to the ball, you have a thirty-foot (9-meter)
putt if your average step is three feet. This is not a magic system
to tell you how hard to hit the putt. It's a system to get you in the
ballpark so you have some idea of how hard to hit the putt.

135 GAUGING SPEED ON THE GREENS

Ann Obermeyer, LPGA Teaching Pro, the Village Club of Sands Point, Sands Point, New York

Being able to control the speed of a putt is essential to becoming a good putter. A good place to start is to walk off the amount of paces you are from the hole. We look at yardages on full shots, yet it is every bit as important on the putting green. While this is not automatic, it will get us close to have the size of the stroke match the length of the putt. For a putt of ten paces, the stroke will be about eighteen inches (45.5 centimeters) forward and back. We are all different, and there are many variables, but walking off the putt and matching your stroke to that distance is a good place to start.

136 THE RIGHT THUMB
Guna Kunjan, PGA Director of Golf, Harbor Links Golf Course, Port Washington, New York

For short puts, take a normal putting grip, with your right thumb straight down on your grip. When you make a putting stroke, note that the right thumb does not twist or turn. This method will square the face of the putter every time.

137 THE LONG PUTTER
Jeff Seavey, PGA Teaching Pro, Samoset Resort Golf Club, Rockport, Maine

I'm an advocate of the long putter and have been since 1988. I feel the ball rolls better with a long putter, rather than the standard putter, because the natural release of the club head produces immediate top spin. To use the long putter successfully, rest the handle of the putter snugly in the center of your chest. Your top hand holds the club to the chest while the bottom freely swings the putter. This approach reduces anxiety, which, in turn, increases confidence. This style of putting is like cheating. It's too easy.

The long putter

138 PUTT LIKE YOU'VE MADE IT A THOUSAND TIMES

Scott Ford, PGA Teaching Pro, North Hills Country Club, Manhasset, New York

We all practice putting to gain confidence. After you've made a good series of putts on the practice green, try to carry that to the course. When you approach the putt, reflect on all the putts you just made. Your attitude should be: "I've made this putt a thousand times. This will be just another one of those thousand. This is easy."

139 FEELING THE WEIGHT OF THE PUTTER

Shawn Baker, PGA Director of Golf, the Greens at Half Hollow, Melville, New York

You should rely on the weight of the putter to move the ball. There should not be a definite hit, but, rather, a smooth stroke as the putter swings to the hole. The ball just gets in the way of a good stroke. As your putts get longer, the size of your stroke should increase. Any hit impulse will make it difficult to feel the distance. A smooth stroke will create a true roll, so the ball will not bounce on its way to the hole.

140 PUTTING AS AN ART

Shawn Baker, PGA Director of Golf, the Greens at Half Hollow, Melville, New York

Putting is an art form. If it were science, we would all putt exactly the same way. Find a style that is comfortable for your own physique. Don't try to putt like someone else, particularly if you're having trouble. There are a variety of ways to roll the ball on the green. We only have to watch the stars in tournaments to see a wide variety of approaches. Experiment until you find a style you like and can trust.

141 BALL POSITION AND LINING UP A PUTT

Matthew Guyton, PGA Teaching Pro, Old Westbury Golf & Country Club, Old Westbury, New York

Lining up the putter blade is essential to starting the putt on line. One important piece of lining the putter blade is where you position the ball in your stance. If you position the ball too far forward, there is a good chance you'll pull the putt as the putter blade starts to rotate to a closed position. If you position the ball too far back in the stance, you will likely push the putt as the putter blade has not quite returned to square. Experiment a little with the ball position to find the best one for you.

142 PUTTING TRICK, PART ONE

Matthew Guyton, PGA Teaching Pro, Old Westbury Golf & Country Club, Old Westbury, New York

After missing some short putts, you may want to take a different approach on your next one. Most of the time we miss the short one because we anticipate where the ball will go before we actually strike it. We move our eyes and head prematurely. To stay steady, try the listening trick: Keep your head steady and your eyes focused on the ball, stroke the putt, and then wait to hear the ball hit the bottom of the cup.

143 PUTTING TRICK, PART TWO
Matthew Guyton, PGA Teaching Pro, Old Westbury Golf &
Country Club, Old Westbury, New York

Another way to make sure you stay steady on short putts is to close your forward eye. What I like about this trick is that it blocks out the hole and the horizon, and lets you just focus on the back of the ball. Make a good, smooth stroke while watching the ball; keep your head steady; and wait to hear the ball hit the bottom of the cup before looking up.

144 PUTTING TRICK, PART THREE
John Schob, PGA Director of Golf, the Huntington Crescent
Club, Huntington, New York

Yet another way to make sure that your head stays steady when you putt is to look at the hole. Assume the normal address position and then turn your head so you see the hole. It may feel weird the first time or two that you use this trick, but after you see a few putts fall, it may well become a way of life. Remember that any "trick" may last a round, a week, a month, a season, or a career.

145 PUTTING TRICK, PART FOUR

John Schob, PGA Director of Golf, the Huntington Crescent Club, Huntington, New York

Another way to make sure your head stays steady when you putt is to close both eyes after you have established your address position. I know this sounds extreme, but this has worked for many players. This is particularly good if you had some very bad experiences putting the short ones. It's the best cure for the yips that I have found. Just close both eyes, make a putting stroke, and listen. Closing both eyes can work for any distance you want to try.

146 THE YIPS

Kevin Harrington, PGA Head Professional, Mount Snow Golf Club, West Dover, Vermont

The "putting yips" is a unique malady that affects good players. When the player tries to putt, a quick and jerky move is made instead of a nice, smooth putting stroke. If you have never heard of the yips or are not sure what I'm talking about, you are very lucky. Please skip the rest of this tip and move on. I am convinced that the yips are caused by bad alignment and bad mechanics over a long period. The first step to curing the yips is to analyze your alignment. This is best done with a professional instructor, but a buddy can be a big help, too. After you have corrected your alignment, it's time to turn to the putting stroke itself. To make a good stroke, you can try these tricks:

1. A three-count after you strike the putt.
2. Close your forward eye.
3. Close both eyes.

147 LOOK AT THE HOLE
Ken Mast, PGA Teaching Pro, the Original Golf School, Mount Snow, Vermont

The yips affect a lot of golfers, especially experienced ones. A good way to rid yourself of the yips is to look at the hole, not the ball, when you putt. Most golfers focus on the ball and forget about the target. Look at the hole when you putt and say good-bye to the yips.

148 HOW TO HANDLE VERY FAST DOWNHILL PUTTS
Jay Campuzano, PGA Teaching Pro, Muttontown Club, East Norwich, New York

Sometimes we have a fast, downhill putt that we just know we'll hit past the hole. To top it off, we may also be downwind. A good way to hit this putt as softly as possible is to address the ball way out on the toe of the putter. Hold the handle of the putter softly and hit the ball toward the toe of the putter. You are then creating a nonsolid hit. The ball will roll softly and hopefully will not sail past the hole. This takes some practice, but it will pay off.

Look at the hole instead of the ball when putting.

149 TEMPO IN THE PUTTING STROKE

Joe Elliott, PGA Teaching Pro, Garden City Country Club, Garden City, New York

Your stroke must have a consistent tempo for you to be a good putter. The putter should be swung at an even pace on the back and forward swing. To help establish that good tempo, practice with a metronome. Set it at a pace you're comfortable with. A song with an easy rhythm in the background, or in your head, is also a great way to smooth out the putting stroke.

150 SOME PUTTING KEYS

John Meckstroth, PGA Teaching Pro, the Original Golf School, Mount Snow, Vermont

1. Keep your body still. The putting stroke does not require a weight shift or extra movement.
2. Keep your eyes still over the ball.
3. Think about the distance of the putt and the length of the stroke.
4. Trust your instincts. We're all athletes, and you should have faith in your own athletic ability.

151 KEEP YOUR HEAD STEADY

Amanda Arciero, PGA/LPGA Teaching Pro, Fresh Meadow Country Club, Lake Success, New York

We all know that to putt well you have to keep your head steady. One of the best ways to do that is to focus on one small spot. Try focusing on one dimple on the ball when you putt. You'll find that you stay very steady and make very solid contact.

152 LINE THE LETTERING ON THE BALL TO THE HOLE

Amanda Arciero, PGA/LPGA Teaching Pro, Fresh Meadow Country Club, Lake Success, New York

The easiest and best way to ensure proper alignment on the green is to line the lettering on the ball to the line of the putt. After you mark the ball, replace the ball on the green so the lettering is directly on the line you wish to start the putt. After you line the lettering, trust it. Often our eyes can play tricks on us. Lining the lettering to the target line is foolproof.

153 USE THE LINE ON THE PUTTER

Greg Pace, PGA Teaching Pro, Huntington Country Club, Huntington, New York

I received a great tip once from Lee Trevino. He suggested that I line up the putter blade using the line on the top or back of the putter, not the face of the putter. The blade may be off a fraction—it can lie to you. The line on the top or back of the putter will always tell you the truth.

154 FOR THE SHORT ONES

Shawn Baker, PGA Director of Golf, the Greens at Half Hollow, Melville, New York

The width of the putter is usually about the width of the hole. On putts under six feet (1.8 meters), aim the line on the top of the putter at the middle of the hole, and then address the ball off-center to allow for the break. If the putt breaks right to left, address the ball on the right side of the putter (not much, just about a half an inch). If the putt breaks left to right, position the ball on the left side of the line. If you can sight the line, you can do this.

155 TRY THE BELLY PUTTER
Shawn Baker, PGA Director of Golf, the Greens at Half Hollow, Melville, New York

A good change for those who have had putting woes is to try the belly putter. The belly putter will give you some feel back without having to go to the extreme of the long putter. After some success with the belly putter, it's pretty easy to go back to the standard-length putter. Sometimes a change of scenery will do you good.

156 EYES OVER THE BALL AT ADDRESS

Keith Newell, Teaching Pro, the Original Golf School, Mount Snow, Vermont

It's beneficial to stand close enough at address so that your eyes are directly over the ball. This helps you easily see the line as you move your head from side to side. It also makes it easy to swing the putter straight back and straight through. In addition, this approach guarantees that you will achieve the exact same address position every time, which is the first step to being consistent.

CHAPTER 8

TROUBLE
SHOTS

157 INTO THE WIND

Don Beatty PGA Director of Golf, Garden City Country Club, Garden City, New York

Playing into the wind requires the ability to hit the ball on a lower trajectory. If you can hit it low, it is much easier to manage because the wind will have less effect on the distance the ball travels. To keep the ball low, take on more club, position the ball back in the stance, and make a low follow-through. Remember what the old Scotsmen say about the wind: "When it's breezy, swing easy."

Playing with the wind at your back sure is easy. With a tee shot, just tee it high and let it fly. Approach shots are different. A wind

behind you will make it more difficult to control the distance you hit your shot to the green. Sometimes the wind will carry the ball, other times it can actually knock the ball down. To best control the distance on the approach shot, try to play a low shot to the green, which is easier to do if there is no bunker in front of you.

159 PLAYING OUT OF DEEP ROUGH

Michael T. Wanser, PGA Teaching Pro, Cherry Valley Golf Course, Garden City, New York

Deep rough will normally close the club face as the club head reaches the ball. To prevent that, it's good to steepen the angle of the club head on the downswing. The easiest way to do this is to position the ball in back in the stance. This ball position will automatically create a steeper downswing. For shorter shots from the deep rough, place a little more weight on your forward foot. That, once again, will steepen the angle of the downswing. The long grass will normally twist the club face a little, so be sure to allow for that.

160 PLAYING OUT OF DEEP ROUGH, REDUX

Tom Herzog, PGA Teaching Pro, the Champions Course, CedarBrook Country Club, Old Brookville, New York

Playing from deep rough is difficult because grass will be caught between the club face and the ball. To minimize the effect of the long grass, stand a little taller at address. This will create a more upright swing and a steeper angle on the downswing. Also use a more lofted club than you would normally need for the shot, as the long grass will have the effect of closing the club face.

161 FAIRWAY BUNKER SHOTS
Shawn Baker, PGA Director of Golf, the Greens at Half Hollow, Melville, New York

Fairway bunkers are bunkers alongside the fairway. The goal is to get out of the bunker and still get some distance. Club selection is very important when it comes to fairway bunker shots. It is best to choose a club with plenty of loft to carry over the front edge of the bunker. If you think a 7 iron will just make it, choose an 8 or 9 iron to give yourself additional loft. To execute the stroke, shorten up on the handle of the club about an inch, play the ball back slightly in the stance, and then try to hit the middle of the ball.

162 BALL IN THE ROUGH, NEAR THE GREEN

Shawn Baker, PGA Director of Golf, the Greens at Half Hollow, Melville, New York

Often the ball will be just a foot or two (30–60 centimeters) off the green, but will be nestled down in the rough. It's very difficult in this situation to hit the ball cleanly with an iron. Try putting the ball out of the rough with a hybrid. The flat sole of the hybrid will help the club slide through the rough and, surprisingly, the ball will come out rolling like a putt. It takes a while to gauge how much swing or stroke you need for the given distance.

163 DON'T AIM AT THE TROUBLE

Scott Ford, PGA Teaching Pro, North Hills Country Club, Manhasset, New York

All players curve the ball, either left to right or right to left. We should play whichever pattern we have established. If the ball tends to curve left to right, you should aim somewhat to the left. One good rule to follow is never to aim the ball at trouble. We never know when the dreaded straight ball will arrive. It's awfully upsetting to see a perfectly hit ball sail into the woods because you overplayed your pattern.

164 PLAYING FROM WET FAIRWAYS

Michael T. Wanser, PGA Teaching Pro, Cherry Valley Club, Garden City, New York

Wet fairways are difficult. (And remember, you always get relief from casual water.) If the fairway is wet, but does not qualify as casual water, you have to play the ball. Try this when the grass is wet: Address the ball holding the club about two inches (5 centimeters) above the turf. If anything, you may hit the ball a little too cleanly doing this. We are trying to protect against hitting behind the ball, resulting in a fat shot and a lot of turf flying everywhere. If the ball is hit too cleanly, you'll still get some distance. If you hit behind the ball, the club head will be stuck in the grass and you will not get any distance.

165

PLAYING THE BUNKERS AT ST ANDREWS, SCOTLAND

Graeme Lennie, Teaching Pro at the Old Course at St Andrews, Scotland

Nothing prepares you for actually being in one of the Old Course's famous deep bunkers. Unlike golf in the United States, the bunkers on the Old Course are one-shot penalties at least. These deep bunkers are "reverted," meaning that blocks of turf or sod are piled up at an acute angle, building a wall that forms the face of the bunker. One reason bunkers were built like this on the Old Course was to keep the sand from being blown out of the pits. There are 112 bunkers on the Old Course.

COURSE
MANAGEMENT

166 MAKE A PLAN
Sandra Jaskol, LPGA Teaching Pro, Old Westbury Golf & Country Club, Old Westbury, New York

It's very important to plan your round. It doesn't have to be written down, but you do need a plan. Before you play, go through every hole on the course. Where should you play your tee shot? What holes should you try to play aggressively, and which ones should you play more conservatively? Are there holes that you always have trouble with? Maybe on those holes, you should change your strategy—consider using a 3 metal wood off the tee, or even a hybrid or an iron. Your strategy should play to your strengths. Remember, Zach Johnson won the Masters in 2007 when he chose to lay up on all the par-5s at Augusta. His strength was his wedge, and he played to it.

167 PLAY THE HOLE LIKE A CHAMPION
Shawn Baker, PGA Director of Golf, the Greens at Half Hollow, Melville, New York

Bunkering and hole designs are planned with back tees and championship players in mind. Whether you are a male or a female playing from forward or a higher handicap set of tees, be knowledgeable about bunker locations and hazards. Try to strategically play a hole to avoid the trouble that may more easily occur on the back tees. Play away from the trouble you may not be able to handle.

Arnold Palmer (Photo courtesy of Bruce Curtis)

168 IF YOU CAN'T REACH THE GREENS
Marcus Munsill, PGA Teaching Pro, Switzerland, Japan, and the United States

If you cannot reach the green on your approach shot, make sure you play a smart shot. Keep your approach shot well short of the bunkers in front of the green. Position your ball so you will have the easiest possible shot to the green. Don't leave yourself a chip or pitch shot where you have to negotiate a huge mound or put yourself in a position where the green slopes dramatically away from you.

169 THE NEXT STROKE
Tom Joyce, PGA Pro Emeritus, Glen Oaks Golf Club, Maiden, North Carolina

I have two simple rules to help me work my way around the course. The first rule is to plan where I want to play my next stroke from. I want the next one to be as easy as possible. My second rule is to plan where I want to be if I lay up—whether it be yardage on the next shot that I like or a plan to leave the ball well short of any trouble. If you're going to lay up, do it well.

170 AVOIDING BIG NUMBERS

Kevin Harrington, PGA Head Professional, Mount Snow Golf Club, West Dover, Vermont

As amateur players, we sometimes allow the bad shot to compound our score. For example, we hit a poor tee shot and have 210 yards (192 meters) to the green. Our ball is in the rough. Usually we are mad and we try to hit the green. This can have a compounding effect on our score if we do not hit the shot we have envisioned. Usually we don't pull off this difficult shot and wind up in a hazard or a bad situation. I try to pick a club to play out of the rough that is easy to hit and will leave me a yardage I like for my next shot. Then I feel I'll have a good chance to hit that shot close and save par. This decision helps to take the bigger numbers off the scorecard.

171 SMART GOLF

Jay Morelli, Director of the Original Golf School, Mount Snow, Vermont

If you make a poor score on a given hole, ask yourself if it was a result of a bad swing or poor shot selection. Every player is going to hit poor shots. We see that all the time in professional tournaments. Mis-hit golf shots happen. Poor shot selection doesn't have to happen. Playing smart golf means playing the shot with the best percentages for success. I don't mind hitting bad shots nearly as much as I mind hitting dumb ones.

172 PLAY THE SHOT YOU KNOW YOU CAN HIT

Paul Rollo, PGA Teaching Pro, Huntington Crescent Club, Huntington, New York

Confidence is such a big part of the game. It breeds good swings. When you have a choice of which club to use or which shot to play, always choose the one you know you are most comfortable with. It's different for every player. One player may choose a wedge to hit a high shot; another may choose a 7 iron from the same position to hit a low shot. Play the shot with the club you know you can hit.

173 LOFT VERSUS DISTANCE

Aaron Mueller, PGA Teaching Pro, Huntington Country Club, Huntington, New York

We're often faced with the choice of loft versus distance when we are selecting a club for a particular shot. In almost all cases, the more lofted club is the better choice. Simply put, the longer the ball stays in the air, the farther it goes. Choosing a more lofted club will also get the percentages in your favor. A mis-hit shot will still get in the air.

174 CLUB SELECTION

Paul Rollo, PGA Teaching Pro, Huntington Crescent Club, Huntington, New York

Choosing the correct club to play a shot is critical to getting your best score. Most recreational players choose a club that they must hit perfectly to reach the green. It is important to take into account that most recreational players will not have a high percentage of solid contact—maybe 75 or 80 percent. Combining less-than-perfect contact with conditions such as wind, low temperatures, and change in elevation will result in choosing more club—using the 7 iron instead of the 8 iron. There will also be less pressure on you to make a perfect swing to get the ball on the green.

175 THE WEATHERMAN
Shawn Baker, PGA Director of Golf, the Greens at Half Hollow, Melville, New York

As Bob Dylan said, "You don't have to be a weatherman to know which way the wind blows." It's good to know which way the wind is blowing before you get to the course. A strong wind coming out of the west may mean you can reach in two shots a green that you cannot normally reach in two. It may mean you cannot reach a hole in two that you normally can reach. If you cannot reach the green, you may want to plan the best place for your pitch shot. Knowing which way the wind is blowing on a given day will help you make a realistic game plan.

176 SIMPLIFY, ALWAYS
Clifford Bouchard, PGA Teaching Pro, Haystack Golf Club, Wilmington, Vermont

Golf is a simple game. We are hitting a ball with a club into a hole . . . and, boy, can we make it complicated! Golfers can go down endless paths that create confusion. Keep your concepts and swing thoughts as simple as possible. Trying to control every part of your swing and your body is impossible.

177 DON'T WORRY
Jay Morelli, Director of the Original Golf School, Mount Snow, Vermont

It's so important to grasp and trust the basics: grip, posture, alignment, and ball position. Get those fundamentally correct and everything else will take care of itself. All golfers have to realize is that golf balls take crazy bounces and the game cannot be 100 percent fair. Take the good with the bad, and always go back to the basics.

178 JUST BEFORE YOU SWING
Kate Baker, LPGA Teaching Pro, Pebble Beach, California, and the Greens at Half Hollow, Melville, New York

Just before you swing, picture the shot you are trying to hit and the area where you are trying to get the ball. This is the direct opposite of focusing on the mechanics of your swing. Imagining your shot produces a smooth swing. Focusing solely on mechanics can make things too complicated.

179 PLAY WITHOUT FEAR
Jay Morelli, Director of the Original Golf School, Mount Snow, Vermont

Golfers are so often afraid of bad shots that they sometimes play timidly, making timid golf swings. You are much better off going ahead and making a committed and strong swing. Commit to the shot and don't even think about what not to do. A nonswing will never produce a good result.

180 GRAVITY IN PUTTING

Greg Pace, PGA Teaching Pro, Huntington Country Club, Huntington, New York

Downhill putts may be treacherous. When you analyze the downhiller, try to see where gravity will take over, and then putt to that spot. In many cases, a thirty-foot (9-meter) putt may only have to go halfway or even less if the greens are very fast. If you think of that same thirty-foot putt as a fast thirty-footer and try to hit it twenty-nine feet, you'll go far past it. If you check where gravity is going to take over, you may only have to hit the putt halfway or even less. Let gravity be your friend.

181 ADJUSTING TO SLOW GREENS

Shawn Baker, PGA Director of Golf, the Greens at Half Hollow, Melville, New York

Adjusting to the speed of the greens is a big part of the game. Finding the greens to be slow, and then leaving putts short all day, makes for a very long day. If you find the greens very slow, try this subtle change: Separate your hands on the handle of the putter. This will give your stroke a little more pop and should help you reach the hole.

182 ADJUSTING TO FAST GREENS

Joe Elliott, PGA Teaching Pro, Garden City Country Club, Garden City, New York

Finding the greens to be fast and hitting the ball past the hole all day can also make for a long day on the greens. If you find the greens very fast, try a few adjustments: Hold the handle of the putter more softly than normal. Address the ball more on the toe of the putter. Hitting the ball on the toe creates a quieter contact.

183 DON'T CHECK THE SCOREBOARD

Kate Baker, LPGA Teaching Pro, Pebble Beach, California,
and the Greens at Half Hollow, Melville, New York

It's so natural to check the scoreboard before you play to see what earlier competitors have scored. But checking the scores generates unnecessary stress. It distracts you from completing your task, which is to play eighteen holes to the best of your ability. It takes away from your focus. So ignore whatever earlier players have posted. Wait until you've finished your round to get excited or upset.

184 TAKING THE PRESSURE OFF THE TEE SHOT

Paul Glut, PGA Director of Golf, Woodside Acres Country Club, Syosset, New York

We've all experienced that very difficult tee shot, out of bounds on both sides. A good way to take the pressure off is to imagine that you've already hit one out of bounds (you haven't) and make believe this tee shot is your second tee shot. The second tee shot, we all know, goes right down the middle. Aim where you want to go, don't worry about where you don't want to go, and swing away. Who says the game is mental, anyway?

185

PLAYING THE ODDS
Shawn Baker, PGA Director of Golf, the Greens at Half Hollow, Melville, New York

Make yourself a promise this season to play the best percentage shot. A good place to start is to keep the driver in the bag more often and use a 3 wood for the tee shot. Another good alternative is to play a highly lofted driver, one with 12 to 14 degrees. Using a lofted driver or 3 metal wood off the tee will greatly increase the percentage of fairways that you reach and greatly decrease the errant shots that result in a big score and a bad day.

186 GETTING THE BALL IN THE AIR

Jayson Lyons, Rockville Links, Rockville Center, New York

It's pretty simple—the longer the ball stays in the air, the farther it goes. When choosing a club, make sure you have one with enough loft. If you have a bare lie and hit a 3 wood, even a well-hit ball will fly low. You are almost always better off choosing a 5 or 7 metal wood if the ball is on bare ground. Not only will the ball go farther, but it is also much easier to hit!

187

TEE UP AWAY FROM TROUBLE

Joe Elliott, PGA Teaching Pro, Garden City Country Club, Garden City, New York

If there is trouble on the right side, most golfers will go to the far left side of the tee box to tee their ball up. That actually makes the tee shot more difficult. The correct and most effective way to avoid the trouble is to tee off on the side of the trouble so you are hitting away from it. If the lake is on the right tee, place your ball on the right side of the tee and aim down the left side of the fairway.

188 TEACHING A CHILD

Kate Baker, LPGA Teaching Pro, Pebble Beach, California,
and the Greens at Half Hollow, Melville, New York

The golf habits children learn often stay with them their entire golfing life. That's why it's so important to get them started correctly. The best gift you can give a young golfer is the correct grip. The grip affects everything—the look of the swing, the pace, the shape, and the strength. A good grip will help the young player develop faster. The swing is simply a reflection of a good grip.

189 SHORT-TERM MEMORY

Tom Herzog, PGA Teaching Pro, the Champions Course,
CedarBrook Country Club, Old Brookville, New York

As golfers, we tend to dwell on what happened on the last hole or the hole before that. It's easy to get down on ourselves if we've made some bad mistakes: a putt left short, a tee shot out of bounds, or one of the many things we know can go wrong on the course. This is the time to forget about those mistakes and move on to the next holes. They are the only ones we can change. Short-term memory loss is a big advantage on the golf course.

190 PLAYING INTO THE WIND

Shawn Baker, PGA Director of Golf, the Greens at Half Hollow, Melville, New York

The wind is probably the biggest variable we have to contend with on the course. Besides learning how to control the trajectory of your flight, you also should show due respect for the wind. It will knock your ball down—it's a matter of physics. Use your imagination when choosing your club. Obviously, the stronger the wind, the more club you will need to reach the target. Remember to have respect for the wind, take plenty of club, and don't force your swing.

191 PLAYING INTO VERY STRONG WIND

Don Beatty, PGA Director of Golf, Garden City Country Club, Garden City, New York

When the wind is blowing hard, you have to get very imaginative. This is the time you should not even consult your yardage book. You may have to hit the 4 or 5 clubs more than if there was no wind. You can't compute that, so disregard the yardage and use your imagination.

192 PLAYING DOWNWIND (FOR ADVANCED PLAYERS)
Don Beatty, PGA Director of Golf, Garden City Country Club, Garden City, New York

The wind will carry the ball. That's a good thing if you have the wind at your back and you're hitting a tee shot. However, it can really complicate things when you are trying to play an approach shot. The wind may carry it farther than you ordinarily would hit the ball. On occasion, it will actually knock the ball down. So when playing downwind on an approach shot, it's best to try to hit the ball with a lower trajectory. It's easier to figure the distance it will travel.

193 DON'T FORGET THE WIND
Scott Ford, PGA Teaching Pro, North Hills Country Club, Manhasset, New York

We have all done it. We hit a beautiful shot, flying straight at the flag, only to have it blown off course. We knew it was a windy day, but we neglected to factor in the wind. This happens sometimes when we are hitting from a hollow or protected part of the course and we can't feel the wind near the green. Get a good picture of the prevailing wind each day and factor that into your plan.

194 USE ONE MORE CLUB
Scott Ford, PGA Teaching Pro, North Hills Country Club, Manhasset, New York

Most golfers—even experts—often leave their approach shots short of the green. The next time you play, try this simple exercise: Hit one more club to the green than normal. I think you will be surprised. First of all, if your hit is not perfect, you will still be on the green, and, second, even if you hit the approach shot perfectly solid, it will only be a little short of the hole. Taking one more club gives you the entire green as a target. Not hitting enough club will only give you the front half of the green as a target.

195 AVOID SUCKER PINS
Shawn Baker, PGA Director of Golf, the Greens at Half Hollow, Melville, New York

Oftentimes, the course will be set up with a few sucker pins that are tucked away in the very corner of the green, behind a bunker. This is when the foolhardy fire away at a flagstick that they cannot get close to. When you see the flagstick tucked away like that, turn your focus to the middle of the green. Hit the ball there and two-putt the green.

196

PUTT THE SHORT ONES PAST THE HOLE

Shawn Baker, PGA Director of Golf, the Greens at Half Hollow, Melville, New York

If you don't reach the hole, the ball cannot go in. We've all heard that a million times. That doesn't make it any less true. This adage really applies to short makeable putts, maybe under ten feet (3 meters), and even a shorter distance for newer players. Putting the ball past the hole on the short ones gives you a chance. If you have ten short putts in a round and reach the hole every time, some will fall. If you leave them all short, obviously you've missed some golden opportunities.

197 ANALYZING THE BREAK OF A PUTT

Guna Kunjan, PGA Director of Golf, Harbor Links Golf Course, Port Washington, New York

The most accurate way to determine the break is to keep your eyes open. If another player is in your line and has to putt first, carefully watch the ball roll. How it rolls will tell you how your ball will react. If you putt and the ball goes past the hole, carefully watch which way it breaks as it rolls. (Many players look away as the first putt misses.) Also, keep your eyes open on a chip or pitch shot that runs by the hole.

198 LESS PRESSURE IN PUTTING

Guna Kunjan, PGA Director of Golf, Harbor Links Golf Course, Port Washington, New York

Often we will have a short birdie putt. We're excited and make too much of it. The extra pressure only makes us try too hard, which will cause a variety of problems with the putting stroke, from grip pressure to looking up too quickly to see where the ball went. A way to take the pressure off is to pretend that the short putt is for a par or a bogey. So relax, remembering that even the best players in the world only make about half of their eight-foot (2.5-meter) putts, and make a good stroke.

199 STAYING FOCUSED
Scott Ford, PGA Teaching Pro, North Hills Country Club, Manhasset, New York

When playing the game, you must remember to stay focused at all times. The period between shots tends to give time to let the mind wander. This creates a lack of confidence. You should be confident and visualize every stroke. If you do hit a poor shot (which every golfer on the planet does), it is important to remain positive. Any type of negative attitude will invariably result in loss of confidence.

200 FAIRWAY BUNKERS
Scott Ford, PGA Teaching Pro, North Hills Country Club, Manhasset, New York

You need a good plan for the long fairway bunker shot. If you're in a fairway bunker 220 yards (201 meters) from the green, chances are that it will take two shots to reach the green. Divide the distance of your shot by two. Two 110-yard shots is usually doable. If you choose to play a more aggressive shot, you run the risk of a serious mis-hit, when it was probably impossible to reach the green anyway. Play your fairway bunker shot to a level position in the fairway so your next shot is in a good place to play from.

201 FAIRWAY BUNKERS WITH A BAD LIE

Paul Rollo, PGA Teaching Pro, Huntington Crescent Club, Huntington, New York

If your ball is in a fairway bunker and you've caught a bad lie with the ball in a footprint or somewhat down in the sand, you have to play intelligently. If the ball is in the sand, you can't possibly

strike the ball cleanly. There is no way to achieve any distance. Play the ball just to get out of the bunker, but make sure you are hitting the ball to a place that will give you a good lie and an easy next shot. Many players try to advance the ball at the flagstick and wind up on the downslope of the bunker in deep grass. The smart play may be to hit the ball sideways to the fairway so you have an easy next shot.

202 DON'T USE A LOB WEDGE ON AN UPHILL LIE

Aaron Mueller, PGA Teaching Pro, Huntington Country Club, Huntington, New York

Often we'll get an uphill lie around the green. Just by addressing the ball, the loft of the club will be increased. The 60-degree wedge may become 64 degrees or more. You will almost always leave your shot short if you play the lob. When you have an uphill lie around the green, stick with the sand or even the pitching wedge to make sure you reach the flagstick.

203 DON'T USE THE LOB WEDGE AGAINST A STRONG WIND (FOR ADVANCED PLAYERS)

Shawn Baker, PGA Director of Golf, the Greens at Half Hollow, Melville, New York

The lob wedge will throw the ball high into the air. If the wind is blowing against you, it's almost impossible to control your distance—you are at the mercy of every gust of wind. Use the sand or pitching wedge instead. The wind will knock the ball down so the ball will not run. The sand wedge against the wind will stop every bit as quickly as the lob without any wind.

204 UNEVEN LIES

Marc Turnesa, PGA Director of Golf, Rockville Links Club, Rockville Centre, New York

The game is a series of adjustments. We have to adjust to wind, temperatures, different lengths of grass, and the like. Our biggest adjustment, however, is the uneven lies, when the terrain is not perfectly level. Two simple ideas will help you make this adjustment. The first is common sense. If you have a sidehill lie with the ball above your feet, shorten up on the handle. The second idea is to take a practice swing (like a dress rehearsal) next to the ball in a similar lie. This will give you some feedback. Do I feel I shortened up on the handle enough? It will also give you some feel for the stroke ahead.

205 THE SIDEHILL LIE WITH THE BALL ABOVE YOUR FEET

Marc Turnesa, PGA Director of Golf, Rockville Links Club, Rockville Centre, New York

This shot resembles a baseball swing. If the ball is above your feet, you'll need to shorten up on the handle somewhat to compensate for the ground being higher than on a level lie. The amount you shorten up depends on the steepness of the slope. Now take a practice swing to check if you have shortened up on the handle the correct amount. Note where the club head touches the turf. It will usually be about in the middle of your stance with this lie. The tendency among most players is to pull the ball, so you have to adjust your target to allow for a pull.

206 THE SIDEHILL LIE WITH THE BALL BELOW YOUR FEET

Marc Turnesa, PGA Director of Golf, Rockville Links Club, Rockville Centre, New York

The challenge in this shot is getting down to the ball. If the ball is below your feet, you should hold the club at the end in order to help you get down to the ground. Widening the stance will also help you get down to the ball. If the ball is well below your feet, you should flex your knees, remembering that the spine angle should remain the same. Take a practice swing to see if you adjusted enough, and note where the club head is striking the turf. It will usually be in the middle of the stance with this lie. The tendency for most players is to push the ball, so you have to adjust your target to allow for a push.

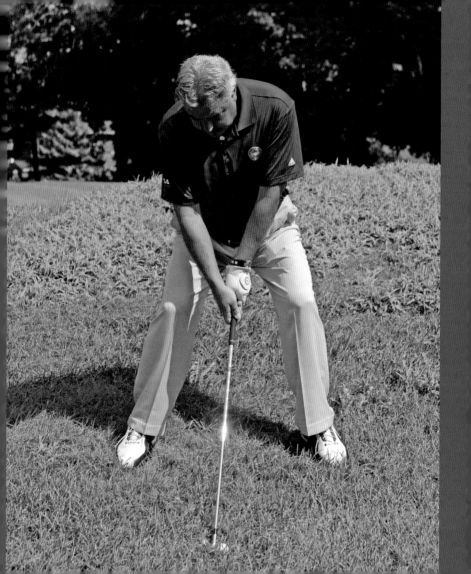

207 DOWNHILL LIE

Marc Turnesa, PGA Director of Golf, Rockville Links Club, Rockville Centre, New York

The challenge with the downhill lie is to get some height on the shot. Just by taking the stance, the club head will lose some loft and the ball will fly lower than usual. You have to play for that. Shorten up on the handle, as the ground will be higher near your back foot. Take a few practice swings. The club will normally hit the turf toward your back foot. That becomes your ball position. Swing the club head down the hill so it follows the contour of the hill. The tendency for most players is to push the ball from this lie, so you have to adjust your target to allow for the push.

208 UPHILL LIE

Marc Turnesa, PGA Director of Golf, Rockville Links Club,
Rockville Centre, New York

There is good news and bad news with the uphill lie. The good news is that it's easy to get the ball airborne as the uphill terrain offers a launching pad. The bad news is that you can hit this shot very crookedly because gravity has your weight on the back foot. Take a few practice swings. No need to choke up: The club head will usually hit the turf in the middle of your stance. Because gravity will keep your weight more on the back foot, play to pull the ball. It's also a good idea to exaggerate your follow-through to "walk up the hill." This will minimize the amount of the pull.

209 IF YOU'RE GOING TO LAY UP, LAY UP

Shawn Baker, PGA Director of Golf, the Greens at Half Hollow, Melville, New York

If you're going to intentionally play the ball short of a hazard, make sure you leave it well short of that hazard. If the 6 iron will leave you five yards (4.5 meters) short of the hazard, use the 7 iron. Making sure you lay up well back eliminates the chance that you might have misjudged the distance. Ironically, it seems that when we are trying to lay up, we often make our best swing. You might actually get a little extra out of the 6 iron and reach the hazard. And the course has so many variables that a gust of wind or some unexpectedly hard ground may increase the distance you hit the ball.

210 LAY UP TO A YARDAGE MARKER

Shawn Baker, PGA Director of Golf, the Greens at Half Hollow, Melville, New York

If you cannot reach the green on a particular shot, think how far you would like your next shot to be. Many players have a favorite club or yardage they would like to have to the green. They would also rather have a full shot to the green than a half shot. If you are 250 yards (229 meters) from the green, you may choose to intentionally hit the next shot 150 yards (137 meters) to leave you 100 yards, rather than hitting the ball 200 yards to have a 50-yard shot left.

211

KNOW WHEN TO HOLD 'EM, KNOW WHEN TO FOLD 'EM

Shawn Baker, PGA Director of Golf, the Greens at Half Hollow, Melville, New York

We are often faced with a choice, to play it safe or to go for it and gamble. Think about it this way: "If I take the chance, will it save me a stroke?" If the answer is no, don't take the chance. If the answer is yes, consider the chance. For instance, if taking a chance by hitting the ball over a pond gets you on the green, it may make sense. If hitting the ball over a pond only shortens your next shot by a few yards, it probably doesn't make sense.

212 DON'T SHORT-SIDE YOURSELF

Scott Ford, PGA Teaching Pro, North Hills Country Club, Manhasset, New York

Short-siding is missing the green on the side of the green where the flagstick is. This leaves you very little green to use for a chip or pitch shot. If the flagstick is tucked into the right side of the green, it's important not to miss the green on the right side. If you miss the green on the right, you'll probably have a lot of long grass between you and the flagstick, making it very difficult to pitch or chip the ball close to the hole. If you miss that same green on the left side, you will have a much easier shot, as you will have plenty of green to use for a chip-and-run or pitch shot.

213 IF YOU DO SHORT-SIDE YOURSELF
Scott Ford, PGA Teaching Pro, North Hills Country Club, Manhasset, New York

If faced with this shot, *make sure you get the ball on the green.* Assume that your chip or pitch will be a little past the hole, but safely on the green. If you try to play too delicate a shot and just hit the very front of the green in an attempt to get the ball close, there is a good chance the ball will fall short. This compounds the original mistake of missing the green on the short side.

PRACTICE
AND
DRILLS

214 CHANGE IS NOT EASY
Jay Morelli, Director of the Original Golf School, Mount Snow, Vermont

Only through practice and drills can you make a change in your game. Decades ago, I took a lesson from Ted Kroll, a three-time Ryder Cup player. He told me my left-hand grip was too strong and my right-hand grip too weak. I worked hard to correct my grip. Ted and I became good friends. Three decades later I asked Ted to take a look at my game. He said that my left-hand grip was too strong and my right-hand grip was too weak. Yes, change is difficult.

215 THE HUMBLING GAME
Jay Morelli, Director of the Original Golf School, Mount Snow, Vermont

The great amateur champion Bobby Jones once said, "Golf is said to be a humbling game, but it is surprising how many people are either not aware of their weaknesses or else reckless of their consequences." Don't be blind to your weaknesses and don't pretend they don't exist. We all have them. Only by recognizing what is wrong with your game can you go about effecting change.

Bobby Jones (Photo courtesy of Bruce Curtis)

216 TAKE NOTES
Jay Morelli, Director of the Original Golf School, Mount Snow, Vermont

Golfers who want to improve practice. It's as simple as that. To get the most from your practice session, buy a small notebook and put it in your golf bag. Jot down the different things you tried, what worked, and what didn't. If you keep this book, over time you will see a pattern of successful strategies emerge. It will save you countless hours and journeys down the wrong road. All players like to tinker in search of the secret, but you'll find the greatest success if you stick to the fundamentals and keep track of what works.

August 25th
2011

My Driver is working great! I got a ᴡ hole in one on the 16th

217 HOW TO PRACTICE PUTTING
Jay Morelli, PGA Director, the Original Golf School, Mount Snow, Vermont

Most golfers go to the practice green and work on ten- to thirty-foot (3- to 9-meter) putts. I feel that time can be put to better use by dividing the practice sessions into two distinct areas. First, you should practice the three- and four-foot (1- and 1.2-meter) putts you can make. Most players miss them because they don't practice them enough. Second, you should then practice getting the longer putts *near* the hole. This is called *lag putting*, and is described in greater detail in tip 221.

218 PRACTICE PUTTING TO A SMALLER TARGET

Jeff Pratt, PGA Teaching Pro, Tam O'Shanter Club, Brookville, New York

This is a good drill to make the hole look larger the next time you play. Find a level spot on the practice green. Putt one ball into another one that is placed one foot (30.5 centimeters) away. Do this until the ball you're putting caroms straight back every time. Then lengthen the putt to two, three, and four feet. When you can do this from four feet with some consistency, you are ready to play. Don't start putting for the hole on the practice green—go straight to the course. The hole will look larger.

219 TAKE A DEEP BREATH (FOR NEW PLAYERS)

Ann Obermeyer, LPG Teaching Professional, The Village Club of Sands Point, New York

New players often are so anxious about learning to play that they actually forget to breathe. If you are taking some instruction, make sure you are relaxed. Take some deep breaths and relax your shoulders. Learning when you are relaxed, with the idea of having fun, is definitely the best and most effective way to learn this wonderful game.

220 LEARN ABOUT YOUR CLUBS (FOR NEW PLAYERS)

Shawn Baker, PGA Director of Golf, the Greens at Half Hollow, Melville, New York

A set of clubs are the tools of the trade. I start out with new players by placing a set of clubs against the wall or the golf cart. I describe what each club does. The metal woods are the longest and hit the ball the farthest. The hybrids are for intermediate distances, while the irons are generally used for approach shots. I explain that the lower-numbered clubs have less loft and are longer, producing longer, more line-drive-type shots. This information is obvious to the experienced player, but it sure helps the new player understand how the game is played.

221
LAG PUTTING
Will Filkins, PGA Teaching Pro, the Original Golf School,
Mount Snow, Vermont

Getting long putts close to the hole is called lag putting. Hitting the putt on line is fairly easy, but hitting the putt the correct distance takes time and practice. Practice by looking at the hole and not the ball. It will help you understand the connection between the size of the putting stroke and the distance you will hit the ball and will make you a more successful putter.

222 PRACTICE ROUNDS

Aaron Mueller, PGA Teaching Pro, Huntington Country Club, Huntington, New York

Practice rounds are designed to give you a feel for the course that you will soon be playing in competition. To get the most out of the practice round, play two or three balls off the tee with different clubs to drive the ball to the best position in the fairway. (I know this is not always possible, but it's great to do if you have the opportunity.) Pitch the ball around the green from several different angles. And don't forget to hit some shots from the sand, since bunkers vary from course to course. The practice round is the chance to learn all about the course. The better you know it, the more prepared you will be when the whistle blows.

223 THE SPLIT-GRIP DRILL
Shawn Baker, PGA Director of Golf, the Greens at Half Hollow, Melville, New York

Here's a terrific drill to help you properly feel the release of the club. It's called the split-grip drill. Separate your hands on the handle so there is some space between your hands—maybe an inch or two (2.5–5 centimeters). Hit a few balls. You'll definitely feel your bottom hand release the club, allowing the forearm of the bottom hand to cross over the forearm of the top hand.

224 USE A MIRROR
Sandra Jaskol, LPGA Teaching Pro, Old Westbury Golf & Country Club, Old Westbury, New York

A good way to practice at home is to make swing improvements in front of a mirror. If you're having trouble shifting your weight, for instance, try to shift your weight properly by looking in the mirror. Visualize the correct motion and repeat it. After you visualize, try to feel it. Then bring that feel to the course or practice area.

225 QUALITY, NOT QUANTITY
John Meckstroth, PGA Teaching Pro, the Original Golf School, Mount Snow, Vermont

For a good and productive practice session, start with a plan. What you are trying to accomplish that day? Imagine a shot you are trying to perfect, a desired distance you would like the ball to go, or a specific club you are trying to master. Practice slowly and remember your goal. Many golfers just hit balls, instead of imagining the shot they are trying to make. Work through your bag hitting all the clubs, and picture the shot you are trying to make. Make sure you go through your pre-shot routine before you swing. This will make for a better, more productive practice session.

226 TOES UP

Jeff Pratt, PGA Teaching Pro, Tam O'Shanter Club,
Brookville, New York

One of the most basic and valuable teaching drills is the "toe-up, toe-up" drill. Start out by making a short swing, hip high on the backswing to hip high on the forward swing. When the club is hip high on both the backswing and the follow-through, the toe of the club should be pointing to the sky. These two positions will point out any flaws, and you can make necessary corrections to create the toe-up position. After creating the correct toe-up positions on the hip high swing, increase the size of the swing until you eventually have a full swing.

227 WARM-UP DRILL
John Gaeta, PGA Teaching Pro, North Hills Country Club, Manhasset, New York

While we all know we should warm up before we play, realistically we don't always have time. A good shortcut is to use a driver, take your normal stance, and center your head over an imaginary ball. Hold the driver waist-high and try to stretch out your lower back. Exaggerate your turn. This may not be as effective as hitting a bucket of balls, but it will help loosen you up before you play.

228 HOLD THE FINISH
Cathy Thiem, Apprentice Teaching Pro, New Hartford, Connecticut

One aspect of your swing to practice is to hold your finish after you hit the ball. Try to hold your finish until the ball lands. Focus on the finish, not the ball or where the ball is going. If you get into a well-balanced finish position, most of the good shots you are looking for will appear more often. When practicing, focus on the solution or movement, not just the ball. Do not be concerned with missed shots or undesired results. The practice tee is where you are allowed to make mistakes.

Warm-up drill

229 THE ONE-PIECE TAKEAWAY DRILL

Shawn Baker, PGA Director of Golf, the Greens at Half Hollow, Melville, New York

A one-piece takeaway simply means that the triangle formed by your arms and shoulders moves all together when you take the club back. To help get the feel for this, practice by placing a long cylinder of Styrofoam or a cardboard box directly in the path of the club head on the backswing. You'll notice how much easier and more powerful it is to move that Styrofoam when you use the big muscles of the arms and shoulders, rather than the small muscles of your hands.

230 PRACTICE LIKE THE PROS
Aaron Mueller, PGA Teaching Pro, Huntington Country Club, Huntington, New York

Do you notice that when the pros practice they try to hit the iron shots from the same place? They put the next practice ball at the end of the divot of the one before. It really minimizes the amount and size of the divots you take, and it's a lot easier on the turf. The course superintendent will appreciate it. You will also find that not taking a new divot with every iron shot is easier on your arms, hands, and elbows.

231 THE LIMBO CHIPPING DRILL
Mary Slinkard-Scott PGA/LPGA Teaching Pro, the Plantation Golf Resort, Crystal River, Florida

To hit solid, consistent chip shots, the club head has to stay low to the ground, particularly on the follow-through. To keep the club head low, picture a bar about a foot off the ground just ahead of the ball. The bar should be much like the bar used in the limbo. The club head should strike the ball and then be able to stay low under the "limbo bar."

232 WORSE BALL
Amanda Arciero, PGA/LPGA Teaching Pro, Fresh Meadow Country Club, Lake Success, New York

I ask my players to play two balls. After they hit two, they play the worse one. If one is hit on the green and one in the bunker, you have to play the ball in the bunker. If you hit one bunker shot close and the next far from the pin, you have to play the farther one. This exercise is terrific for emphasizing the importance of every single stroke. After you hit a good one, you have to dig in and do it again.

233 BETTER BALL
Kevin Harrington, PGA Head Professional, Mount Snow Golf Club, West Dover, Vermont

My players enjoy this exercise much more than worse ball. The players hit two balls and then play the better one. Hit again and play the better one again. This exercise is terrific at showing how well you can really play. It's a great confidence builder.

234 PLAY WITH JUST A FEW CLUBS

Amanda Arciero, PGA/LPGA Teaching Pro, Fresh Meadow Country Club, Lake Success, New York

A great way to explore your golf imagination is to play with just a few golf clubs. Try 3 clubs: a 3 wood, a 7 iron, and a sand wedge. You will be surprised how well you can do. Drive with the 3 metal wood, use the 3 metal wood or 7 iron for the fairway shot, the 7 iron and sand wedge around the green, and the 3 metal wood to putt.

235 SHORT GAME DRILL

Ron McDougal, PGA Director of Golf, Old Westbury Golf & Country Club, Old Westbury, New York

This is a good drill to help you gauge distances for chips and pitch shots. Lay a towel on the edge of the green and practice landing a chip shot on the towel. Gradually move farther away from the green. Note how far the ball rolls out as your distance from the green increases. Practice this with different clubs to see the different ratio of carry to roll as the loft of the various clubs increases.

236 ROTATION DRILL

Shawn Baker, PGA Director of Golf, the Greens at Half Hollow, Melville, New York

Stand with your feet pointing toward the target, beside the ball. Ball position is best opposite the toes. Rest the club handle against your thigh, with the club head behind the ball. Make a good grip and proceed to the backswing. The amount of turn will be limited, but the midsection of your body will feel the built-up tension. As you start to unwind through and past the ball, you'll realize that you cannot stop this action. It will carry you through to a poised position at the follow-through. This drill will develop a *swing* as opposed to a *hit*.

237 THE L TO L DRILL
*Amanda Arciero, PGA/LPGA Teaching Pro, Fresh Meadow
Country Club, Lake Success, New York*

Head out to the backyard one day with your clubs, a ball, your video recorder, and a tripod. Set up the recorder so it will capture your practice swings. Focus on swinging naturally, and take several swings. How's your setup? Do your arm and club form the letter "L" on your backswing at the 9 o'clock position and a backward "L" at the 3 o'clock position during the follow through? This is called the L to L drill, and if you don't see those "Ls," work on leveraging your swing. This will lead to more power!

238 STAY "QUIET" ON CHIP SHOTS

Sandra Jaskol, LPGA Teaching Pro, Old Westbury Golf & Country Club, Old Westbury, New York

You should keep your body still on chip shots to ensure solid contact. To get the feel of staying quiet, try to hit some practice chips while standing wedged inside the legs of a bag stand. This will eliminate any excess motion and promote solid contact.

239 BALANCE DRILL

Sandra Jaskol, LPGA Teaching Pro, Old Westbury Golf & Country Club, Old Westbury, New York

Try this experiment to check your balance. Without a ball, swing the club to the top of the backswing. Drop the club and then try to put a finger on your left shoulder. It sounds simple, but it's not that easy to do. Many people fall backwards! Good balance is a key to a good, powerful, repeating swing. Balance should be good both front to back and side to side.

240 PRACTICE WITH YOUR FEET TOGETHER

John Schob, PGA Director of Golf, the Huntington Crescent Club, Huntington, New York

In most lessons, instructors try to eliminate something from a golfer's swing, rather than adding something. Before problems develop, try this: At the range, hit the first twenty-five practice balls with your feet together. Use an easy club, maybe a 7 iron. You will find that your body is not moving much, and you will feel only your arms and shoulders doing most of the work. Your ball contact will improve immediately. Now gradually spread your feet apart and see if you can keep that same feeling. Let your hips and knees move as a result of your swinging arms. This drill will help you develop consistency, good balance, and tempo.

241 FEEL THE LAG (FOR ADVANCED PLAYERS)

Jay Morelli, Director of the Original Golf School, Mount Snow, Vermont

Lag is initiated by lower-body rotation from the top of the swing. It is most commonly felt in the angle between the hands and the forearms in the downswing. To get the feel, try this exercise: Attach both ends of a bungee cord to the top of your golf cart. Flip the head of an iron so the toe is pointing down, and secure the loop end of the bungee cord around the club head. Feel the resistance of the club head while it's above your hands as your hands pull toward impact.

242 AIMING DRILL
John Gaeta, PGA Teaching Pro, North Hills Country Club,
Manhasset, New York

Being able to aim is huge. Correct alignment makes for good swings. If your aim or alignment is poor, only by compensating will you be able to produce a good result. When you make a good swing and the ball doesn't head in the direction where you were aiming, check your alignment. Place a club shaft down across your feet to see where you were originally aiming. Our eyes can play tricks on us. To correct poor alignment, practice with a shaft across your toes aimed properly. Good alignment will begin to become second nature.

243 GREENSIDE BUNKER DRILL
Aaron Mueller, PGA Teaching Pro, Huntington Country Club, Huntington, New York

To be a good bunker player, you must swing through a divot of sand, knocking the sand and ball out of the bunker. A good way to practice is to draw a circle of sand in the bunker, about the size of the divot. (You can only do this in practice.) Now make some swings trying to throw a divot of sand out of the bunker. After you get the feel for this, put a ball in the middle of the divot and make the exact same swing. If your ball is going to leave the bunker, you have to get in the habit of knocking out that divot of sand.

244 THE DOLLAR BILL DRILL

Sandra Jaskol, LPGA Teaching Pro, Old Westbury Golf & Country Club, Old Westbury, New York

A Scottish pro once told me you'll never be a good bunker player until you can bury a dollar bill about an inch deep in the sand, just about where the divot of sand would be on your bunker shot. So, set the ball in the area of the dollar bill. Swing the club, skimming the sand so the sand and ball come out, but the dollar bill stays in the same place. It's a neat trick that may cost you a few dollars, but it's worth it!

The setup for the dollar bill drill.

245 PUTTING FOR DISTANCE CONTROL

Paul Rollo, PGA Teaching Pro, Huntington Crescent Club,
Huntington, New York

The most important aspect of good putting is distance control. To improve distance control, try this fun drill. Start at the center of the practice green. Try to putt the ball toward the fringe without quite reaching it. You can try this drill with three or four balls. Also, putt from several distances, perhaps ten feet (3 meters), then twenty feet (6 meters), and then thirty feet (9 meters). It's great practice and fun, too, if you can do it with a friend. Putting to the fringe of the green, rather than the hole, will free up your mind so you're not overly concerned with the line. But it allows you to concentrate on the distance you're putting.

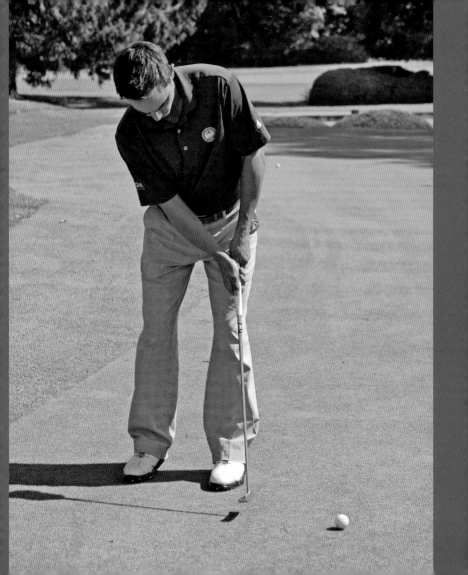

246 CHIPPING

Shawn Baker, PGA Director of Golf, the Greens at Half Hollow, Melville, New York

To chip consistently, you must strike the ball on the downswing. Most recreational golfers try to scoop the ball, resulting in poor contact. A great drill to learn to chip the ball on the downswing is to place several balls about a foot (30 centimeters) or so behind the ball you are playing. In order to hit the target ball and miss the balls behind it, you must swing the club head at an angle from high to low. You will find that placing more weight on your forward foot will help make you successful with this drill. This setup puts you in a position to create the necessary angle to hit the ball on the downswing.

247 EASY POWER

Shawn Baker, PGA Director of Golf, the Greens at Half Hollow, Melville, New York

To gain a few more yards on your tee shot without swinging harder, makc a wide takeaway. Place a golf glove under your lead armpit and squeeze it just tightly enough to prevent it from dropping. Your lead arm is now connected to your torso. Now take some swings. The club head will remain low and extended in the backswing. This connected takeaway widens your arc, which will add distance and height to your tee shots.

248 CORRECT PRACTICE

Shawn Baker, PGA Director of Golf, the Greens at Half Hollow, Melville, New York

Most golfers go to the practice area and hit drivers for the entire session. While the driver is an important practicing club, it will do little to improve your score. Keep varying your clubs when you practice. Try switching back and forth. Hit some drivers and then try some short irons and some fairway metal woods. You can duplicate a golf round right on the range. Go through the clubs you use during a typical round. Varying the clubs you use in practice will make for a good, realistic session that will improve your game.

249 STEP DRILL FOR PROPER SEQUENCE

Shawn Baker, PGA Director of Golf, the Greens at Half Hollow, Melville, New York

This is a good drill for players who come over the top of the ball, rather than hitting it squarely. Take a normal backswing, and then move the front foot next to the back foot. In the forward swing, move that foot once again so you are stepping into the shot, much like a baseball pitcher or a tennis player. This move ensures that you will initiate the swing with the lower part of the body with a proper weight transfer.

250 SEEING THE LINE OF A PUTT

Shawn Baker, PGA Director of Golf, the Greens at Half Hollow, Melville, New York

Your eyes can play tricks on you. Sometimes when we stand over a putt, we may think we see the line correctly, and yet a small distortion or an incorrect perception may make a huge difference. Here's a good test: Select a level ten-foot (3-meter) putt. Determine the line, and then place a coin or other marker directly on that line halfway to the hole. Now stand over the ball. Don't hit the putt, but look up to see if the coin has "appeared" to move. If so, your perception is off. This can be corrected by using an intermediate target or the letters on the ball to line up.

251 THE SMALL PRACTICE HOLE
Shawn Baker, PGA Director of Golf, the Greens at Half Hollow, Melville, New York

Some courses cut a smaller-than-standard cup on the putting green. The theory is that after you putt to the very small cup, the regulation cup will look larger. The problem is that very few putts on the practice green will fall into that small cup. The net effect is that practicing into the smaller hole gets poor results and may be counterproductive. None of us needs to make fewer putts while practicing.

252 THE SEVEN-BALL PUTTING DRILL

Amanda Arciero, PGA/LPGA Teaching Pro, Fresh Meadow Country Club, Lake Success, New York

Gauging and controlling speed on the greens are acquired skills. It takes practice to get the feel for how hard to hit the ball a given distance. A great drill to develop this feel is to use seven balls. Start at one side of the green and putt the first ball to the far fringe. Then try to leave each putt short of the one before it. Repeat this drill in a few different directions. This is a great drill when you are playing a new course. It's also a great way to acquire the feel for a course, since the speed of the greens changes every day, even hour by hour.

253 ACQUIRING FEEL WITH A PUTTER

Amanda Arciero, PGA/LPGA Teaching Pro, Fresh Meadow Country Club, Lake Success, New York

Golf instructors can teach mechanics, but not *feel*. Acquiring feel takes time and patience. This drill will help. Line up seven balls about a yard apart, moving away from the hole. Draw an imaginary line around the hole (about the size of a bushel basket). Putt the first ball into the imaginary circle. Keep moving back to the last ball. As you are gradually moving away from the hole, notice how each stroke has a different feel.

PUTTING ALIGNMENT
*Amanda Arciero, PGA/LPGA Teaching Pro, Fresh Meadow
Country Club, Lake Success, New York*

To increase consistency and confidence in your putting stroke, place two clubs on the green, parallel to each other. Be sure to place the clubs only as wide as your putter head. Try to get a level putt and have the path they create aimed at the hole. Set the ball between the clubs and stroke the putt. If the putter head strikes the shafts, you know that the putter is not going straight back and straight through. If the clubs are lined up properly and you stroke the putt correctly, the ball will go into the hole.

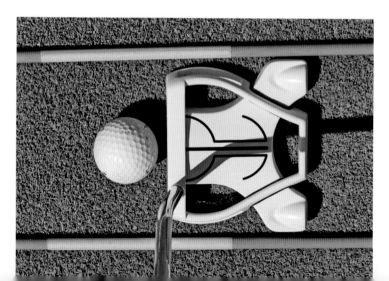

255 PRACTICE ROUTINES
Shawn Baker, PGA Director of Golf, the Greens at Half Hollow, Melville, New York

A very good time to practice is *after* you play. Sam Snead, one of the best players ever, would warm up before he played, then play his round. After the round, he would have a quick drink or a bite to eat and then practice. Practicing after the round is productive because the shots you hit well or poorly are fresh in your mind. It's also good to think about the poor shots you made during the round and then work them out.

256 PREVENT SWAYING
Scott Ford, PGA Teaching Pro, North Hills Country Club, Manhasset, New York

Moving the body laterally, or swaying, on the backswing gets you out of position to make a solid, repeating swing. To prevent the sway, place a golf ball under your back foot. As you begin the backswing, the ball will keep you from going to the outside of your back foot. To swing correctly, you should be in balance, with pressure more toward the instep, rather than the outside of the foot.

257 PREVENT FLYING ELBOWS

Scott Ford, PGA Teaching Pro, North Hills Country Club, Manhasset, New York

Some golfers *disconnect*, meaning their arms do not turn with their bodies. This will cause flying elbows. Here's a drill to reduce this: Place a towel across your chest with each end under each armpit. Or place a club head cover under each arm while practicing. This will keep your arms connected to your body throughout the swing and produce more consistent results. Another way to correct flying elbows is to place a towel under your lead shoulder. This is called a connected swing.

258 A DRILL FOR THE CORRECT GOLF GRIP

Scott Ford, PGA Teaching Pro, North Hills Country Club, Manhasset, New York

Draw a short line on your index finger, just above the second knuckle, and another just below the third knuckle (use a thin, dry-erase marker). When you look down at your grip, these lines should be parallel to each other. If the lines are not parallel, your grip is incorrect.

259 TOE UP TO TOE UP DRILL
Douglas Miller, PGA Professional, Gold Coast Golf Center,
Woodbury, New York

When hitting practice balls, practice with your feet together (touching). Hit balls using only the shoulder turn and swinging the hands. With your feet together, your body cannot move left or right or up and down. You will just pivot on that spot. This drill will improve your balance and the feeling for swinging the club head.

260 TURN YOUR BODY BACK, TURN YOUR BODY THROUGH
Don Beatty, PGA Director of Golf, Garden City Country Club,
Garden City, New York

Most errors in the golf swing begin with the backswing. Golfers incorrectly begin the backswing with their arms and hands, rather than with their body turn. Try this exercise to fix this tendency. Start with your arms folded across your chest and emphasize bending from the waist. From this position, turn your body back, and turn your body through, while keeping your head still. This motion will help you feel that the backswing and the downswing begin with your big muscles, not your arms and hands.

261 CURE THAT SLICE
John Schob, PGA Director of Golf, the Huntington Crescent Club, Huntington, New York

Here's a great drill to cure the slice: Hit some balls with your back facing the target. This sounds tougher than it is. Use an easy-to-hit club. Tee the ball up. Address the ball with your back to the target. This drill will promote a better (more inside to straight) path for the ball. It will also promote a better release of the club head.

262 NO BIG DEAL, LIFT THAT HEEL

John Schob, PGA Director of Golf, the Huntington Crescent Club, Huntington, New York

Most golfers incorrectly place too much weight on their back foot at impact. This robs the golfer of power and solid contact. At impact, your weight should be on the front foot, with your lower body rotated toward the target and your back heel off the ground. Practice this correct impact position by first swinging to the top of your backswing. Now, in slow motion, begin your downswing in one smooth motion—your arms, upper torso, and lower torso all synchronized at the same speed. Stop at impact, and you will see and feel the correct impact position. This position is the same in all sports with respect to where your body and arms should be at the point of impact. When you swing the club, be athletic and allow your body to rotate through impact. No big deal, lift that heel!

263 FEEL THE PROPER IMPACT

Michael T. Wanser, PGA
Teaching Pro, Cherry Valley
Club, Garden City, New York

Having your weight on your front leg at impact is absolutely critical for good golf shots. A good drill to feel proper impact position is to hit balls from impact. Put all your weight on your front leg and pick your back heel up off the ground so that the rear toe is on the ground for balance. Position the ball off your left foot. Your center is now positioned forward and this will allow for a descending blow. Simply swing back and then rotate your body to the target as your club swings through. Finish with your chest facing the target. This drill will ensure that you are on your front leg at impact.

264 TEE-IN-THE-MOUTH DRILL

*Mary Slinkard-Scott, PGA/LPGA Teaching Pro, the
Plantation Golf Resort, Crystal River, Florida*

If you have a tendency to laterally move too much to the right during your backswing, here is a tip that will help. Place a golf tee in your mouth as a reference point. If your head stays fairly steady during the backswing, the tee will always be steady.

265 TENNIS BALL DRILL

*Kate Baker, LPGA Teaching Pro, Pebble Beach, California,
and the Greens at Half Hollow, Melville, New York*

Hold a tennis ball in the palm of your hand and squeeze it repeatedly with your fingers until they get tired. Repeat this drill a few times a week with both arms and you will build strong forearms.

266 USE A COIN

Kate Baker, LPGA Teaching Pro, Pebble Beach, California, and the Greens at Half Hollow, Melville, New York

Place a coin on the putting green directly behind the ball. Then narrow your focus on the coin with the sweet spot of your putter. As you stroke over the middle of the coin, hit the back of the golf ball with the middle of the putter head. This exercise really helps you to zone in and hit the ball out of the middle of your putter head.

267 HIT YOUR IRONS OUT OF THE SWEET SPOT

Kate Baker, LPGA Teaching Pro, Pebble Beach, California, and the Greens at Half Hollow, Melville, New York

To achieve consistency in your iron play, you have to hit the ball out of the middle of the club's sweet spot. Attach a paper circle on the club face to see whether your golf balls are coming out of the center of the club or not. If you are hitting it out of the middle of the club, the indentations formed in the circle will be grouped closely around the center of the circle on your club face.

268 HOW TO MAKE THE HOLE SEEM LARGER

Kate Baker, LPGA Teaching Pro, Pebble Beach, California,
and the Greens at Half Hollow, Melville, New York

Have you ever had one of those rounds of golf when the hole looks like a large cup and all the putts just drop in? Wouldn't it be great if it was always like that? Sadly, with golf, the opposite may be true: Sometimes you can't buy a putt, no matter how much money you have. All you can do is watch the Golf Channel and see how the pros do it, take lessons from your PGA teaching pro, and practice, practice, practice.

269 COIL UP FOR POWER

Sandra Jaskol, LPGA Teaching Pro, Old Westbury Golf & Country Club, Old Westbury, New York

To get more power and distance, practice with a medium-sized rubber ball between your legs to feel the rotation of your upper body uncoiling above a stable, planted lower body. This springlike effect will keep you more centered over the ball while maximizing your coil with explosive power and speed.

270 SEQUENCE OF MOTION

Sandra Jaskol, LPGA Teaching Pro, Old Westbury Golf & Country Club, Old Westbury, New York

The golf swing motion is very much like that of an underhanded/ sidearm toss of a tennis forehand. The only difference is that the club swings in a different arc, or path. Imagine tossing the club to the target sidearm from the top of your swing in order to get your weight shifting and hips turning first, so that the shoulders, arms, and hands will follow and release the club to the target—in that order.

271 MYTH #1: KEEP YOUR LEAD ARM STRAIGHT

Douglas Miller, PGA Professional, Gold Coast Golf Center, Woodbury, New York

Most golfers are under the impression that they must keep their left arm—that is, the lead arm (for right-handers)—straight. This is often misunderstood to mean ramrod stiff. There is no place for unnecessary tension in the swing. The left arm should get long on the backswing as the right arm gets long on the follow-through. This happens naturally. Neither arm should be stiff. Two great players have naturally bent left arms: Ed Furgol, who won the U.S. Open in 1954, and Calvin Peete, who won the Vardon Trophy for lowest scoring average in 1984.

272 MYTH #2: PULL DOWN WITH YOUR LEAD HAND

Douglas Miller, PGA Professional, Gold Coast Golf Center, Woodbury, New York

Golf is a two-handed game. Each hand does half the work. Pulling with the left hand (for right-handed players) will leave the club face open at impact and create a pushed shot. Allowing both hands to act naturally, and not trying to have one hand or the other dominate the swing, will let the club face rotate back to square, as it should. So let both your hands swing the club!

273 MYTH #3: KEEP YOUR HEAD BEHIND THE BALL

Douglas Miller, PGA Professional, Gold Coast Golf Center, Woodbury New York

You really can't *keep* your head anywhere. Your head is on the top of your spine and will follow wherever your spine takes it. In the perfect swing, your head may move slightly back on the backswing and slightly forward on the forward swing. The swing should be rotational so there will not be a lot of side-to-side motion. Concentrate on a good rotation and don't worry about keeping your head back.

274 MYTH #4: IT'S A LEFT-HANDED OR RIGHT-HANDED GAME

Douglas Miller, PGA Professional, Gold Coast Golf Center, Woodbury New York

As I've said, golf is a two-handed game. Great players have noted that they have a certain "feel" that one hand dominates their particular swing. In reality, the hands should operate as one single unit. They should work together. Try to have equal pressure and equal "feel" in each hand.

NUTRITION

275 PLAYING GREAT ROUNDS

Jay Morelli, Director of the Original Golf School, Mount Snow, Vermont

So often golfers talk about playing a great round for thirteen or fourteen holes, only to have the round fall apart at the last few holes. There was a time when I would have thought their swings abandoned them or perhaps faulty course management caused the weak finish. Now I ask, "What did you eat and when?" I have found that poor eating habits are directly correlated to poor performance, particularly when it comes to not being able to finish the round. So many golfers simply run out of gas.

276 WEEKEND GOLFER DON'TS
Dr. Harry Haroutunian, Sports Medicine Specialist, Palm Desert, California

The weekend golfer normally starts the golf weekend with the Saturday-evening ritual with friends. This includes a couple of cocktails late in the afternoon, a nice big steak on the grill with a glass of wine, then some more wine, dessert, coffee, a nice snifter of cognac, and perhaps a cigar to top off the evening. After tossing and turning all night trying to digest the evening's feast, he gets up at 5:30 to make a 7:05 tee time. Obviously, this won't work.

Avoid overeating the night before a golf game.

277 EAT HEALTHILY BEFORE YOUR ROUND

Dr. Harry Haroutunian, Sports Medicine Specialist,
Palm Desert, California

A huge don't is eating improperly before you play. The weekend golfer grabs a Danish and a cup of coffee. Fired by caffeine and sugar, our friend manages a successful start for the first four or five holes, and then the floor falls out from under him. His blood sugar drops, and a voracious hunger announces its arrival. His concentration wanes. His hands sweat and shake, and he notices some tension in his shoulders. He looks in the golf bag to find a candy bar (located perilously close to the DEET bug repellent). He devours it, and the sugar spike-and-plummet cycle starts all over again.

This is not the best way to start your day.

278 CONTROL YOUR BLOOD SUGAR

Dr. Harry Haroutunian, Sports Medicine Specialist,
Palm Desert, California

Control of your blood sugar has short- and long-term benefits. In the short term, it has positive benefits on your energy level, mental acuity, ability to relax and concentrate, physical endurance, and hunger. Maintaining steady blood sugar, combined with proper hydration, will give you the best chance for top performance on the course and pretty much anywhere else. In the long term, it will also greatly decrease your chance of developing diabetes and cardiovascular disease.

279 BEFORE YOU PLAY
Dr. Harry Haroutunian, Sports Medicine Specialist, Palm Desert, California

Eat light and avoid excessive alcohol and caffeine the night before you play. This will give you an enormous advantage in the next morning's match. You'll awaken feeling refreshed and not famished. A little stretching, a hot shower, and you're good to go. A cup or two of whole-grain cereal with low-fat milk and sliced fruit or a protein drink will provide sustaining fuel until midmorning.

280 DECAFFEINATE
Dr. Harry Haroutunian, Sports Medicine Specialist, Palm Desert, California

Most of us need a few cups of coffee to get going in the morning. While this may provide a nice pick-me-up on the way to work, it is not at all good for keeping the nerves calm when you try to play golf. The best thing you can do is fool yourself by having a cup of decaf coffee. The second-best thing you can do is have a cup of half regular and half decaf. The third-best plan is to drink only one cup of regular coffee. And, of course, a glass of water at the turn is much better for a good back nine than another cup of coffee.

281 DURING THE ROUND
Dr. Harry Haroutunian, Sports Medicine Specialist, Palm Desert, California

A low-carbohydrate, high-protein energy bar is a great boost for that fifth- or sixth-hole slump. (Another energy bar on the back nine will come in handy, too.) If you must eat at the ninth hole, try a high-protein, low-carbohydrate snack. Avoid salty snacks and any products made with white flour or white sugar. Choose whole-grain bread if you are having a sandwich. A good choice would be a light salad that includes shrimp or turkey.

282 GOLFERS HAVE TO EAT
Janet Carl, Director of Golf/Women's Golf Coach, University of Cincinnati

Studies at our school, the University of Cincinnati, have shown that golfers have to have fuel to stay strong enough to play. Players should have a healthful snack. You can either nibble throughout the round or have a snack every four holes. A good example would be a bag of nuts (sans salt), a piece of fruit, or a granola bar.

283 GOLFERS NEED TO HYDRATE

Janet Carl, Director of Golf/Women's Golf Coach, University of Cincinnati

Studies at our school also illustrate how important it is to stay hydrated when we play golf (and for our overall general health). It's important to drink water or a hydrating sports drink before you play and to continue to drink water as you play. This may seem like a lot, but to stay healthy and hydrated you should drink sixteen ounces (45 grams) of water every four holes.

PHYSICAL CONDITIONING

284 KEY COMPONENTS
Larry Feldstein, American Sports & Fitness Association (ASFA) Certified Professional Trainer

To play golf successfully, there are four elements of fitness that you should develop: strength, flexibility, cardiovascular endurance, and balance. These are the basis of any well-rounded fitness program. Improving your golf game requires more than just playing, and you do not have to spend hours in the gym. A program with these components will help to increase lean-body mass, reduce body fat, lower blood pressure, and increase strength, flexibility, and balance.

285 INCREASE STRENGTH
Larry Feldstein, American Sports & Fitness Association (ASFA) Certified Professional Trainer

Developing muscular strength and power will help generate increased club head speed, which will result in greater distance. A full-body strength-training program that concentrates on the core muscles of the body is advised. This should be done two to three days a week with one to three sets of eight to fifteen repetitions per exercise. Use weights that you can easily handle.

286 INCREASE FLEXIBILITY
Larry Feldstein, American Sports & Fitness Association (ASFA) Certified Professional Trainer

You can increase the range of motion in your shoulders, trunk, lower back, legs, and arms with ten minutes of stretching every day. Make sure that prior to stretching you spend three to five minutes warming up your muscles to prevent injury. As you develop greater flexibility, try to increase your stretching over time. This will substantially increase your club head speed.

287 CARDIOVASCULAR CONDITIONING

Larry Feldstein, American Sports & Fitness Association (ASFA) Certified Professional Trainer

Cardiovascular conditioning is necessary to keep your energy level up during your round of golf. Try to do twenty to thirty minutes of walking, jogging, cycling, swimming, ice skating, or whatever aerobic activity you choose. These activities should be done three to five times a week. Increasing the duration, frequency, and intensity of the activity will lead to marked improvement in your breathing, which, in turn, will help your game and settle your nerves.

288 LISTEN TO YOUR BODY FOR BALANCE

Larry Feldstein, American Sports & Fitness Association (ASFA) Certified Professional Trainer

Normal balance depends on information from the inner ear, sight, touch, and muscle movements. The interaction of these alerts us to where our body is during an activity and helps us maintain the desired positions for golf.

289 GOOD EXERCISE: DUMBBELL CHEST PRESS
Larry Feldstein, American Sports & Fitness Association (ASFA) Certified Professional Trainer

1. Place your upper back, shoulders, and neck on an exercise ball. Make sure your knees are bent at a 90-degree angle with your hips parallel to the floor.
2. With your hands shoulder-width apart, slowly lower a dumbbell in each hand until your upper arms are parallel to floor.
3. Slowly press dumbbells back to the starting position.
4. Repeat.

290 GOOD EXERCISE: DUMBBELL WEIGHT PRESS

Larry Feldstein, American Sports & Fitness Association (ASFA) Certified Professional Trainer

1. Lie on your back with your legs on top of the exercise ball. Make sure your knees are bent.
2. Hold dumbbells in each hand, just above your chest, with your palms facing forward.
3. Lift the weights straight up above your shoulders.
4. Hold the position for three counts and then lower the weights. Repeat.

291 GOOD EXERCISE: DUMBBELL ROW

Larry Feldstein, American Sports & Fitness Association (ASFA) Certified Professional Trainer

1. Place your right knee and hand on an exercise ball with your back parallel to the floor and your left arm extended with a dumbbell in hand.
2. Raise your left elbow to just under your chest.
3. Lower the dumbbell to the starting position. Repeat.

Dumbbell Row

292 GOOD EXERCISE: BALL LEG CURLS

Larry Feldstein, American Sports & Fitness Association (ASFA) Certified Professional Trainer

1. Lie on your back with your legs extended and your calves and feet on an exercise ball.
2. Slowly pull the ball toward your buttocks until it almost touches your derriere.
3. Hold the ball for two counts and return to the starting position.
4. Repeat.

293 GOOD EXERCISE: KNEE EXTENSIONS

Larry Feldstein, American Sports & Fitness Association (ASFA) Certified Professional Trainer

1. Place your upper arms, shoulders, and neck on an exercise ball. Make sure your knees are bent at a 90-degree angle and your hips are parallel to the floor.
2. Extend one knee to straighten the leg.
3. Hold for a count of two and return to the starting position.
4. Repeat with the opposite leg.
5. Repeat, alternating legs.

294 GOOD EXERCISE: CRUNCHES

Larry Feldstein, American Sports & Fitness Association (ASFA) Certified Professional Trainer

1. Place your lower back and shoulders on an exercise ball. Bend your knees at a 90-degree angle, your hips

parallel to the floor. Cross your hands on
your chest.

2. Slowly curl your upper body forward in a crunch,
   pulling your belly button to your spine.

3. Repeat.

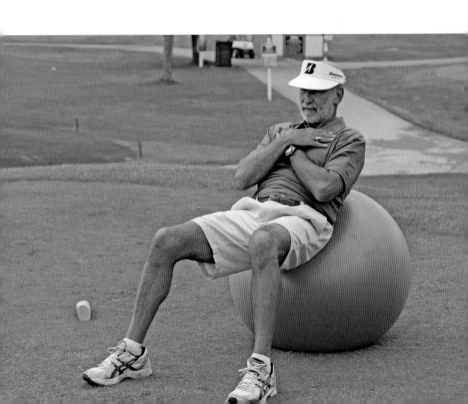

295 GOOD EXERCISE: DUMBBELL SHOULDER PRESS

Larry Feldstein, American Sports & Fitness Association (ASFA) Certified Professional Trainer

1. Sit on an exercise ball with your back straight.
2. Hold two sets of dumbbells slightly above shoulder level with palms facing away from your body.
3. Raise your arms and shoulders upward with the dumbbells moving in line with your ears and over the center of your head.
4. Slowly return to the starting position and repeat.

296 GOOD EXERCISE: SQUATS

Larry Feldstein, American Sports & Fitness Association (ASFA) Certified Professional Trainer

1. Place an exercise ball between a wall and the curve of your lower back.
2. Stand with your feet shoulder-width apart. Then bend your knees and lower yourself about ten inches (don't go farther than is comfortable), your shoulders level and hips square.
3. Hold for three seconds and then stand. Repeat.

Dumbbell
Shoulder
Press

297 GOOD EXERCISE: LATERAL DELTOID RAISE

Larry Feldstein, American Sports & Fitness Association (ASFA) Certified Professional Trainer

1. Sit on an exercise ball with your back straight.
2. Hold dumbbells at a 90-degree angle, with palms facing each other and elbows next to your body.
3. Raise the dumbbells by lifting your elbows, maintaining the 90-degree angle until your arms are parallel to the floor.
4. Focus on using the muscles on the side of the shoulder.
5. Slowly return to the starting position and relax shoulders. Repeat.

298 GOOD EXERCISE: REAR DELTOID RAISE

Larry Feldstein, American Sports & Fitness Association (ASFA) Certified Professional Trainer

1. Sit on the ball and bend forward slightly from the hips.
2. Hold the dumbbells at your sides with your shoulders relaxed.
3. Raise your bent elbows to the rear and outward, squeezing the shoulder blades together.
4. Slowly return to the starting position, relax your shoulders, and repeat.

299 GOOD EXERCISE: HAMMER CURLS

Larry Feldstein, American Sports & Fitness Association (ASFA) Certified Professional Trainer

1. Sit on the exercise ball with your back straight.
2. Hold the dumbbells at your sides with your palms facing your body. Keep your shoulders relaxed and your elbows against the side of your body.
3. Curl the dumbbells to the front of your shoulders.

Rear Deltoid Raise

THE
MENTAL
GAME

300 SMELL THE ROSES

Karl Obermeyer, PGA Director of Golf, the Village Club at Sands Point, Sands Point, New York

The great Walter Hagen said it best: "Smell the roses along the way." The sport of golf is played on the best venue. No football field, baseball stadium, or basketball court can compare to the beauty of a golf course. Take the time to take it in. It makes poor shots not so bad and good shots even better.

301 KNOW THYSELF
Amanda Arciero, PGA/LPGA Teaching Pro, Fresh Meadow Country Club, Lake Success, New York

You have to know what swing tendencies you have on the course, and you only acquire that knowledge by playing. You have to play a lot of golf. Put your game under pressure and see how you react. For instance, you may find that under pressure you tend to hit the ball to the right. The next time you are under pressure, figure a way to prevent the ball from going to the right. It's all about knowing yourself.

302 THAT WINNING FEELING
Jay Morelli, Director of the Original Golf School, Mount Snow, Vermont

Once you get used to winning, it becomes easier the next time you compete. A good step to developing that winning mind-set is to play in events you know you can win. This goes against the idea of stepping up in class to play against the best possible players. But there is no substitute for the feeling of winning.

303 LAUGH

Jay Morelli, Director of the Original Golf School, Mount Snow, Vermont

To handle pressure, you have to keep a sense of humor. Golf is just a game, and even the best players sometimes have difficulties. If you are too tight and take the game too seriously, you are doomed to failure. Stay loose and learn to laugh at yourself—it's the only way to survive and have fun in this most impossible of games.

304 GOLF IS A GAME OF DOING
Jay Morelli, Director of the Original Golf School, Mount Snow, Vermont

Many golfers are very concerned with the don'ts—that is, what not to do. Golf is a game of making the correct swing and a game of doing. To become a better player, you have to understand what you must *do* to get the ball in the hole. The ultimate don't is just standing there, doing nothing. If you just stand there, you can't be doing anything wrong, but you're not doing anything right, either. Good golf is a series of swings and motion.

305 LET SCIENCE DO THE WORK FOR YOU

Jay Morelli, Director of the Original Golf School, Mount Snow, Vermont

Golf companies have spent millions of dollars researching the best golf club and ball design. Golfers should learn one swing and apply it to the fourteen clubs in their bag. Golfers find it hard to believe that they should make the same swing with a 5 iron that they make with a pitching wedge. The instinct is to swing harder with the longer clubs. Scientists in white lab coats have studied these facts: The 5 iron will go farther than the 8 iron without your helping it!

306 STATISTICS

Paul Glut, PGA Director of Golf, Woodside Acres Country Club, Syosset, New York

Tour players keep track of their statistics and so should recreational players. Knowing where your strengths and weaknesses lie is a valuable tool to make your practice time more effective. Take a few minutes to chart your game. Track all shots, particularly those around the green. Tracking your round will highlight the areas of the game you should focus your practice and instruction on. You'll find that the easiest way to improve your game is to improve those short-game statistics.

307 THE ART OF GOLF
Sir Walter Simpson, from The Art of Golf *(1887)*

"The average golfer must be allowed to theorize to some extent. It is a necessary concession to him as a thinking animal. . . . On the other hand, if he does not recognize 'hitting the ball' as his business, theory as his recreation, he becomes so bad a player that he nearly gives up."

308 THE FRESH START
Paul Glut, PGA Director of Golf, Woodside Acres Country Club, Syosset, New York

How often do we hear, "I was terrible on the front nine, but great on the back" or vice versa? There is some barrier or relief players feel when they change nines. It's as if you're given a fresh start. A good way to increase your "fresh starts" is to divide the course into three- to six-hole units, rather than two nines. This is *the* head game, and this little trick can take the pressure off waiting for the tenth tee.

309 A MENTAL APPROACH TO PUTTING

Kate Baker, LPGA Teaching Pro, Pebble Beach, California, and the Greens at Half Hollow, Melville, New York

I just had a student of mine, a highly competitive amateur, ask for a simple putting tip. I suggested this: For all putts inside five feet (1.5 meters)—which most players place a lot of pressure on themselves to make—focus on not missing. I have an inner conversation with myself on every putt. What do I need to do to make this putt? This places the focus on hitting the putt with the correct speed and on the intended line with a free-swinging stroke. The positive approach of trying to do something is much more effective than trying not to make a mistake.

310 TALK TO YOURSELF

Jay Morelli, Director of the Original Golf School, Mount Snow, Vermont

A good way to handle pressure situations is to actually verbalize what the shot ahead calls for. Do this on every shot. It's a routine that will take some of the panic out of the moment. Describe the situation out loud: "I have 138 to the front, 147 to the pin, should be a perfect 6 iron." This will help you focus on the process, not the result. Verbalizing the shot will help relieve pressure. After you verbalize, just try to make a good swing.

311 STAY IN THE PRESENT

Kate Baker, LPGA Teaching Pro, Pebble Beach, California, and the Greens at Half Hollow, Melville, New York

To play your best, you have to stay in the present. It's that feeling of being in the zone, which is actually a heightened sense of awareness of the situation. Forget what happened on the last hole and don't start thinking about the holes ahead. Focus solely on the task at hand—the next stroke.

312 MENTAL TOUGHNESS

Jay Morelli, Director of the Original Golf School, Mount Snow, Vermont

It has been said that the game of golf is played in the six inches (15 centimeters) between the ears. We spend a lot of time learning our swing and how to play certain shots. We spend very little time learning how to deal with the mental side of the game. What do we do on the first tee with twenty people watching? What do we do going to the last hole when we're in the lead? Let's start by doing all the thinking before we start our pre-shot routine. This includes how you want to play the shot, the conditions, and any swing thoughts. Once this is done, you start your routine, which should be the same every time. Think about nothing when you swing. This will be hard to do at first, but rely on the fact that you have already processed the needed information.

Arnold Palmer (Photo courtesy of Bruce Curtis)

313 RELY ON YOUR SWING
Karen Merritt, Golf Pro, North Salem, New York

Everyone gets nervous—that's a given. The best way to handle pressure is to keep it simple. A pressure situation often will get you flustered, so that is the time to go back to the swing thoughts that were successful in other tournaments. Since you have achieved success with those swing thoughts before, you know they will work again. To handle pressure, rely on your swing keys, ignore the distractions, and give it a ride!

314 SWINGING THROUGH THE HITTING ZONE

Jay Morelli, Director of the Original Golf School, Mount Snow, Vermont

A very common problem in golf is not completing the swing, whether it is a driver or a short putt. You should commit to keeping the club swinging through the hitting zone. If you decelerate in the hitting zone, a poor shot will result. In the case of putting, this deceleration is referred to as the yips. This can happen with all clubs. It's always wise to swing fluidly through to your finish.

315 REMEMBER TO BREATHE PROPERLY

Karl Obermeyer, PGA Director of Golf, the Village Club at Sands Point, Sands Point, New York

Even professional golfers go through an entire round and forget to breathe properly. When your breathing becomes shallow, it limits the amount of oxygen in the lungs. Subsequently, the blood going to the extremities has little oxygen, which results in shaky legs, light-headedness, and the like. Cleansing, deep, diaphragmatic breaths keep the blood oxygenated. So remember to take deep breaths, especially when the pressure is on and you need that great shot or putt.

316 THINK POSITIVELY
Jay Morelli, Director of the Original Golf School, Mount Snow, Vermont

We all talk to ourselves on the course. After a few bad shots, it's very easy to get down on yourself and have that conversation turn negative. "My round is ruined," "I'm a terrible golfer," "Why do I even bother?" Make a conscious effort to restructure these pessimistic thoughts. The internal conversation can just as easily go like this: "Everyone hits a few bad shots—that's the game. I usually do come back and I will this time, too."

317 RELAXATION

Shawn Baker, PGA Director of Golf, the Greens at Half Hollow, Melville, New York

The golf swing has very little room for error. We all know that. Any tension can make it impossible to have the club face square up at impact. So it's always wise to do a head-to-toe scan and release any tension in your body before you tee off. In the middle of a round, you might also want to do an inventory of any of your body regions that may be tense, and take a moment to release that tension. Common areas for tension are the neck and shoulders. We have all seen the Fred Couples shoulder roll. Give it a try.

318 BE TARGET-ORIENTED

Karl Obermeyer, PGA Director of Golf, the Village Club at Sands Point, Sands Point, New York

Recreational golfers rarely appreciate the value of internalizing a clear picture of where they want the shot to go. Particularly when there's trouble, such as water or trees, the average golfer tends to think in terms of avoiding the hazard. This is negative thinking. The smart play is to eliminate the image of the trouble spot and visualize the fairway or green that represents the target. Think about the positive, what you need to do, rather than what you want to avoid.

319 PLAY YOUR OWN GAME
Jay Morelli, Director of the Original Golf School, Mount Snow, Vermont

We are always paired with golfers who play better or worse than we do. Play your own game. Players of lesser ability are also trying to have fun. Playing with players better than you can be intimidating. Don't pay any attention to the fact that you may be the shortest hitter. It will only hurt your game. Don't get caught up in comparative golf. Even if you play poorly, nobody cares. The other players are so wrapped up in their own games that they don't even notice yours.

320 USE A TRIGGER
John Gaeta, PGA Teaching Pro, North Hills Country Club, Manhasset, New York

A common problem faced by recreational golfers is freezing over the ball. Ideally, you should engage in a pre-shot routine. In reality, most recreational golfers don't have the discipline of professional players to create and then stick to a good pre-shot routine and repeat the same sequence before every shot. But you should have a cue, like a forward press, to help the swing get started.

321 FOCUS ON THE POSITIVE

Jay Morelli, Director of the Original Golf School, Mount Snow, Vermont

Don't focus on not hitting the ball in the water! Pick out a place where you are trying to hit the ball and let that be your focus. If there is an out-of-bounds area on the right, pick out a target down the left side to aim the ball. Create a positive image of what you want the ball to do, not what you are trying to avoid. Golf is a game of positive focus, not a game of avoidance. Meanwhile, if there is one thing I am certain of in golf, it is that negative thinking definitely works. If you think that the shot will not come off, it won't. If you fret about the pond on the right, you'll hit into it. If you think you'll miss that three-footer (a 1-meter shot), you will. Work at keeping your thoughts positive and have faith that your swing or putting stroke will produce the desired result.

322 CONFIDENCE

Mary Slinkard-Scott PGA/LPGA Teaching Pro, the
Plantation Golf Resort, Crystal River, Florida

Confidence is that intangible element that separates the champs from the others. We have to have the ability to believe we can play our best, regardless of how the round is going. Golf can be inherently unfair. Golf balls take some weird and unfair bounces. Mental toughness means accepting those unfair bounces as the nature of the game and moving on. We must have the belief that the next shot will be a good one, and we have to have the mechanics and swing to hit that good shot.

323 OLD HABITS DIE HARD

Jay Morelli, Director of the Original Golf School, Mount Snow, Vermont

Most golfers usually fall into three or four bad habits over their entire golf life. These habits tend to repeat themselves over and over again and are the product of the body looking for a less stressful way of swinging the club—in other words, we get lazy! The quickest way to get rid of bad habits is to be aware of them. It's a well-known fact that tour players maintain a diary to keep track of what type of mis-hits they are having and how that relates to a particular swing flaw. When we play a lot of golf, we can often miss what's right in front our faces. Write to remember and your golf slumps will be short-lived!

324 STAYING IN THE GAME

Jay Morelli, Director of the Original Golf School, Mount Snow, Vermont

All rounds have an ebb and flow. A mediocre start does not mean a mediocre round. Eventually, you'll find the rhythm and start to play well as long as you keep trying. All great players know and accept that. I think the most satisfying rounds are the one where you start poorly but then recover and play the last few holes at your very best and post a good score. Often the great recovery rounds give your game a momentum that carries over to the next rounds.

325

TAKING A LESSON
Sandra Jaskol, LPGA Teaching Pro, Old Westbury Golf & Country Club, Old Westbury, New York

When teaching a lesson, the instructor will give the player an analysis of what can be improved and some drills or homework to make those improvements. Then the player must practice. When you practice, work on the drills the instructor suggested. Many players will go to the practice tee with the best of intentions to perform those drills, but oftentimes the player will change the focus to how the ball is being hit. Stick with the drills and don't worry about where the ball is going.

326 TEST YOUR SHORT GAME
Stevie Hovey, PGA Rules Expert, the Original Golf School,
Mt. Snow, Vermont

A good way to get a handle on what kind of player you could and should be is to try this exercise. Count how many times during a round of golf it takes you more than three shots to hole out when you are less than fifty yards (46 meters) from the green. (Most golfers can easily get the ball on the green and two-putt from fifty yards and in.) Deduct that number from your score. The new number is what you should score. So practice that short game.

327 THE BEST LESSON I EVER HAD

Jay Morelli, Director of the Original Golf School, Mount Snow, Vermont

I was on Ben Hogan's staff years ago. One of our treats as staff members was that once a year we would go to Fort Worth and meet with Mr. Hogan. I asked him once what he thought about when he was about to hit a shot. I expected a technical answer. He said he thinks about where he wants to play his next shot from and what type of shot he must play to put the ball in that position. I did not think this tip had significance. He challenged our group to ask ourselves that question before each shot in the coming season. The result is that my game improved two levels in that one season.

Ben Hogan (Photo courtesy of Bruce Curtis)

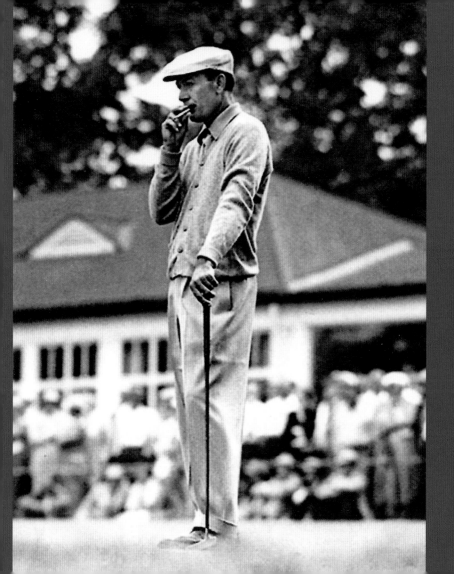

328 TAKING THE PRESSURE OFF
Ron Johnson, PGA Teaching Pro, Somerset, New Jersey

We often play a fantastic shot and have a relatively short putt, maybe eight or nine feet (2.4–2.7 meters), for a par or a birdie. We then tend to attach too much importance to making that putt. Even the best players in the world don't make all of them. In fact, even the best make less than 50 percent from that range. So take the pressure off yourself. All you can do is read the break, relax, and just try to make the best stroke you can.

329 BEING YOUR OWN BEST FRIEND

*Kate Baker, LPGA Teaching Pro, Pebble Beach, California,
and the Greens at Half Hollow, Melville, New York*

In order to be a winner, we demand perfection from ourselves. Perfection, however, does not mean you will win. Winning is the combination of a great many things. One of those things is the ability to be your own best friend. It is okay to be stubborn and have a great desire to win. That is necessary in any sport. But beating up on yourself is counterproductive. When times are tough on the course, be gentle with yourself. Become an encouraging person by your side.

330 LET THE ATHLETE PLAY

Ron Johnson, PGA Teaching Pro, Somerset, New Jersey

In my forty years of teaching, it seems as if we have gone from a game of learning and playing as an athlete to a game where the once-athlete has been overtaken by analysis—so much so that the athlete suffers from PBA: paralysis by analysis. I would recommend to anyone who has played golf, and has the basic fundamentals to play golf on the course—where every shot is different, where the target changes, where the wind is a factor—to play a round with one club to increase the need for imagination and creativity. Play golf and have fun doing it!

331 FOCUS ON THE PROCESS

Mary Slinkard-Scott, PGA/LPGA Teaching Pro, the Plantation Golf Resort, Crystal River, Florida

Many golfers on the women's tour focus solely on the score. Of course, that's important. But even more important is the process. Players should focus on their fundamentals, on their course management, and on playing one shot at a time. Players can get immersed in what score was just made and what score they anticipate on the holes ahead, rather than bearing down and playing the one shot right in front of them. The score will take care of itself if you work on one shot at a time.

332 DRAW A LINE

Amanda Arciero, PGA/LPGA Teaching Pro, Fresh Meadow Country Club, Lake Success, New York

It is easy to do too much thinking, standing over the ball at address. A good way to correct that is to stand behind the ball, looking at the target. Do all your planning and thinking there. Draw an imaginary line behind the ball. After you have done all your planning and thinking behind the ball, cross the line and just do it. After you cross the line, you are an athlete in a sport, just swinging away.

333 STAY COOL
Jay Morelli, Director of the Original Golf School, Mount Snow, Vermont

In pressure situations, it is easy to lose your cool. To stay cool, make an intelligent observation of the conditions. Think of what shot will work best for you. Draw from your experience and, of course, from your common sense. If you do this analysis properly, choose the correct club, and play the best type shot for the situation, your confidence will grow and you'll feel more mentally prepared. Pressure is self-induced. No one cares about your game except you. Other golfers are too worried about their own games and swings.

334 REMEMBER, GOLF IS A GAME
Jay Morelli, Director of the Original Golf School, Mount Snow, Vermont

We play games because they are fun. If your golf game is no longer the fun time it used to be, take a break. Walk away from it for a couple days, weeks, months—however long it takes for you to rediscover the sport for the good time it is supposed to be.

EQUIPMENT

335 THE FLEX OF THE GOLF SHAFT

Clifford Bouchard, PGA Teaching Pro, Haystack Golf Club, Wilmington, Vermont

The flex of the shaft of your golf club is based on ability, swing speed, and strength. Players with greater ability, swing speed, and strength tend to benefit from a stiffer shaft flex. Yet softer-flexing golf shafts do improve distance for all players. The trade-off for a softer shaft is control and contact. All players should start with the stiffest golf shaft available for control. Then, try progressively softer shafts until there is a loss of control or contact.

336 YOUR SET OF CLUBS
Jay Morelli, Director of the Original Golf School, Mount Snow, Vermont

The length of a golfer's set of clubs should be based on talent, not height. Many good, tall players have benefited from standard-length clubs. Talented, short players have gained valuable distance with longer clubs. Fitting clubs to your body height is important when you are just starting out. As a player progresses, the length of the club is more of a personal preference to attain the desired results of maximum distance and control.

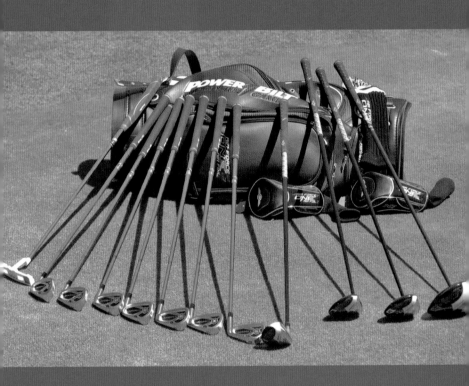

337 FIDDLE WITH YOUR SET MAKEUP

Mike Acerra, PGA Head Teaching Pro, Plandome Country Club, Plandome, New York

As you get older, you don't want to fiddle with the swing that has been useful to you for decades. But you may want to consider fiddling with the makeup of your set of clubs. Take that 3, 4, and 5 iron out of the bag and replace them with 3, 4, and 5 hybrids. As we age, we are more likely to get loft from our clubs, not our swing. And remember, anyone who tells you they play better at fifty-five than they did at twenty-five wasn't very good at twenty-five.

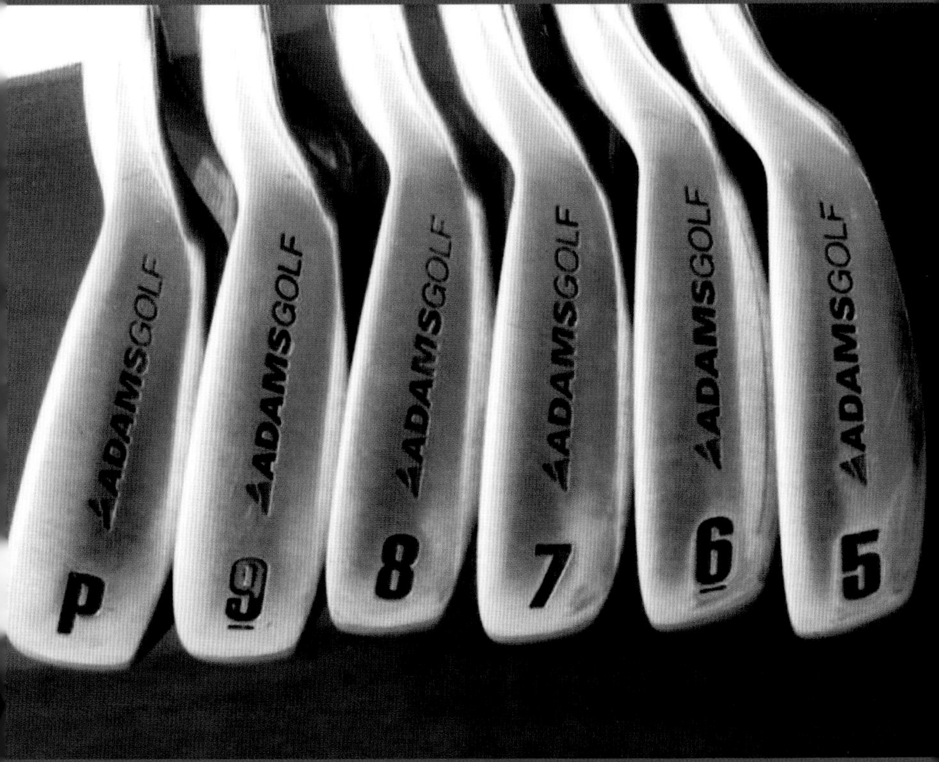
ADAMSGOLF
P
ADAMSGOLF
9
ADAMSGOLF
8
ADAMSGOLF
7
ADAMSGOLF
6
ADAMSGOLF
5

338 THE GOLF SHAFT
Jay Morelli, Director of the Original Golf School, Mount Snow, Vermont

The golf shaft is the key element to a golf club. The shaft is basically a spring. It will bend or spring through the force created by the power of the swing. If the shaft is too stiff for a given player, it will not flex enough to add to the speed of the club head. If the shaft is too flexible, it will spring too much and the player will lose control of the club head and then, of course, the ball. A professional can help find the best combination for any golfer. The shaft should be flexible enough to maximize club head speed, yet firm enough to provide control.

339 THE RIGHT PUTTER FOR YOU

Michael Shank, PGA Head Professional, North Shore Country Club, Glen Head, New York

There is no more important club in your bag than the putter. It should be properly fitted to you personally. To achieve good putting posture, stand tall with your shoulders, back, and chin up. Now bend your elbows and plant your upper arms on the front corners of your rib cage with your hands out in front of you. Internally rotate your arms so your palms are facing the sky. Then take a putter in your hands in this position so the end of the grip points to your belly button. Give yourself a touch of knee flex and bow over at the waist, keeping your back flat and the putter in front of your belly, until the putter head hits the ground. The correct putter length will fall directly under, or about one inch (2.5 centimeters) outside a line drawn down from your eyes to the ground.

340 THE CORRECT PUTTER LENGTH

Tom Herzog, PGA Teaching Pro, the Champions Course,
CedarBrook Country Club, Old Brookville, New York

The most overlooked club in the bag to fit properly is the putter. Most of my students use a putter that is too long. This usually causes the player to address the ball with the toe of the club in the air and standing too far away from the ball, which creates an excessively rounded putting arc. Cutting the putter down to the correct size allows the player to have the putter lie evenly on the ground while getting closer to the ball. This allows the player's eyes to be positioned over the ball and directly over the intended line of the putt, improving accuracy and solidness of contact.

341 PUTTER FITTING

Michael Shank, PGA Teaching Pro, North Shore Country Club, Glen Head, New York

Eighty percent of players are putting with a putter that is too long. The best way to be properly fit for a putter is to go to a professional who has the right fitting system. One thing to watch out for when cutting the putter down is that the head will feel a lot lighter. Cutting clubs down will also affect the balance. That's why it's so important to find the right professional with a good fitting system.

342 FITTING IRONS
Sandra Jaskol, LPGA Teaching Pro, Old Westbury Golf & Country Club, Old Westbury, New York

Irons are accuracy clubs. When getting fit for irons, the first consideration should be accuracy. Distance is not an important factor. Considerations should be the following: lie, shaft flex, length, and shaft type. The best style club head would be a perimeter-weighted design, as they allow better results for off-center contact.

343 SELECTING A DRIVER

Tom Herzog, PGA Teaching Pro, the Champions Course,
CedarBrook Country Club, Old Brookville, New York

The three most important clubs in your bag are the driver, the putter, and the sand wedge. The driver obviously starts the hole. You should choose one that you know you can keep in play. The driver should have plenty of loft, maybe 11 or 12 degrees. Remember that the longer the ball stays in the air, the farther it goes. A driver with loft also goes straighter. It will act more like a 3 metal wood. The driver is a position club. Don't be fooled by a driver that can hit a few feet farther, but only one out of three tries. In golf we have to chase the foul balls.

344 KEEP THE TOOLS CLEAN
Jim Bearden, PGA Teaching Pro, West Islip, New York

It's easy to properly prepare to play, and part of that preparation is cleaning your clubs properly. They can be cleaned with some warm water, a soft brush, and a towel. Looking down at a mud-caked club on your first iron shot of the day just doesn't give you a positive picture, and, worst of all, you'll know in the back of your mind that you haven't done all you could have to prepare to play.

345 REGRIP YOUR CLUBS

Tom Herzog, PGA Teaching Pro, the Champions Course,
CedarBrook Country Club, Old Brookville, New York

Having new handles put on your clubs is a very inexpensive way to make sure you have done all you could to play your best. If the handles are slippery, it's very hard to feel that you can confidently hold the club. This will certainly make the player hold the club more tightly, which increases tension. Slippery grips create uncertainty that you should not have to deal with.

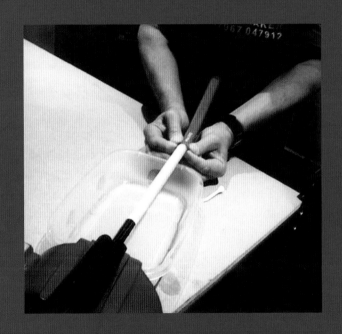

346 GOLF GLOVES

Jay Morelli, Director of the Original Golf School, Mount Snow, Vermont

The golf glove is designed to make it easier for the golfer to achieve a proper and secure grip on the handle of the club. To retain quality, it is best to keep the original package, and store the glove in it after every round. Wear marks on the glove can tell you if you have the correct grip. Wear marks high in the palm show that the club is not being held enough in the fingers. Holding the club high in the palm restricts the automatic hinging of the wrists on the backswing and follow-through.

347

GOLF BALL FITTING

Jay Morelli, Director of the Original Golf School, Mount Snow, Vermont

The newest innovation is using a golf ball that is best suited to your own game. Not all of them are just white and round. Golf balls have different characteristics. The best way to determine the golf ball for you is to go to a fitting where a professional can determine both swing speed and launch angle. The following is a list of recommendations from Bridgestone, one of the best golf ball companies:

1. If you generate more than a 105 mph club head speed and you are looking for maximum distance without sacrificing greenside performance, then the Tour B330 is the ball for you.

2. If you generate more than a 105 mph club head speed and are looking for a softer feel and increased spin greenside, then the Tour B330-S is the ball for you.

3. If you generate a club head speed that is more moderate (less than 105 mph) but you still demand the performance of a urethane-covered ball, then the B330-RX is for you.

4. If you generate a club head speed that is less than 105 mph but demand the ultimate in soft feel and spin control, then the B330-RXS is for you.

5. If you have moderate swing speed and are a high-spin player who has trouble with slices and hooks, the 3-piece, Surlyn®-covered e6 golf ball will improve your accuracy and maximize your distance.

6. If you have moderate swing speed, but prefer the performance of a two-piece distance ball, yet do not want to sacrifice the softness and spin of a urethane cover, the e5 is the ball for you.

7. If you have a higher swing speed and want maximum distance, then the e7 golf ball is the choice for you.

348 GRIP SIZE

Jay Morelli, Director of the Original Golf School, Mount Snow, Vermont

The diameter of the handle of your club can determine how you play. The handle must be thin enough to make the proper grip—mostly in the fingers. If the handle is too thick, the handle of the club will be too much in the palm. Thin grip diameters promote more active hand action and club head release. Thick diameters tend to reduce the amount of hand action. You should consult a PGA golf professional or an experienced club maker to make sure you have the correct grip size.

349 CHOOSING A LOB WEDGE

Jay Morelli, Director of the Original Golf School, Mount Snow, Vermont

A lob wedge has a lot of loft and is designed to hit short, high shots. There may be a big difference in their playability. If the course you play has firm turf, you should choose a lob wedge with a lot of loft and not much bounce. (Bounce is measured by the shape and size of the sole of the club.) Have a professional fit you so the club fits the type of course you normally play. A 60-degree wedge with 4 to 6 degrees of bounce suits most courses and situations. You have to invest plenty of time with the lob to become proficient with it.

350 THE GOLF BAG
Jay Morelli, Director of the Original Golf School, Mount Snow, Vermont

This may not seem important, but you should keep your golf bag in good shape. Many golfers carry around more golf balls than they would need in an entire season. Make a practice bag or simply discard those golf balls you'll never use. Check to see if there are any old granola or candy bars lingering in the corners of the bag. Make sure your bug spray is not past its expiration date. The golf bag should have the items necessary to get you around the course. Keep it clean and current.

THE GOLF SCHOOL

www.thegolfschool.com ♦ 877-344-PUTT (7888)

CANDACE HENDRIX

351 SHOE CARE
Jay Morelli, Director of the Original Golf School, Mount Snow, Vermont

Let's face it, you're on your feet for five hours. You must have a good pair of golf shoes. They should fit comfortably and be clean. Remember that looking sharp is part of the game, and it helps when you hit a few crooked shots. Use shoe trees so the shoes retain their shape, and have a least two pair of golf shoes so you can alternate.

352 SUNGLASSES
Jay Morelli, Director of the Original Golf School, Mount Snow, Vermont

Even though there is no rule against them, most pro golfers don't wear sunglasses. They can be difficult to get used to unless you've been wearing them for a long time, and many golfers report having trouble with depth perception and contrast when wearing them. If you're worried about sun exposure, which could lead to cataracts and other eye diseases, wear a sun visor or look for sunglasses with a high nanometer rating that you can wear comfortably.

CADDY
TIPS

353 ABOUT YOUR CADDY

Jay Morelli, Director of the Original Golf School, Mount Snow, Vermont

The caddy not only carries your bag, but, officially, he or she is the only one allowed to give you advice on the course. A good caddy will know the challenges the course has to offer, hole yardage, strategies for each hole, pin placements, and more. Caddies are not usually employed by the club or resort, but are self-employed. PGA and LPGA rules dictate that the golfer and the caddy walk the course while the caddy carries the player's bag.

354 KNOW YOUR PLAYER
Keith Meskic, Tam O'Shanter Club, Brookville, New York

Good caddies have to be very observant. They have to know the player's game: her strengths, weaknesses, and tendencies. The key for the caddy is to gain the player's trust and confidence, which comes from knowing the greens, surroundings, yardages, and rules. Caddies have to have confidence in their own abilities. If they don't, the player will know.

355 THE BASICS
Keith Meskic, Tam O'Shanter Club, Brookville, New York

The player-caddy relationship varies so much that you can't generalize about it. Some players rely heavily on the caddy for motivation as well as yardages and help reading the greens. Some just want a reliable person to carry the bag who will not incur a penalty. The basic rules on the PGA Tour, though, are simple: Show up, keep up, and shut up. Some players just don't want a cheerleader.

356 KNOW THE RULES

Caddies from the Garden City Country Club, Garden City, New York

Golf tournaments create excitement and tension. When players are in the heat of competition, they often forget the most basic rules. A good caddy must know the rules even better than the player so the caddy can safeguard the player against mistakes and rules infractions. The caddy has to anticipate the next move by the player and remind the player of the rules. The officials and referees will help, if asked, but the responsibility to follow the rules is solely the player's, with the help of the caddy. I don't think any of us will forget how Dustin Johnson lost the PGA Championship in 2010 because he grounded his club in a bunker on the last hole.

357 SPOTTING THE BALL

Keith Meskic, Tam O'Shanter Club, Brookville, New York

Most golfers turn away when they hit an offline shot. That's the time you should really follow the ball. A tee shot straight down the middle is easy to find; a crooked one is not. As the ball travels toward trouble, carefully mark an object directly behind where the ball lands—a tree, a bush, a bunker, and the like. Walk down that line, and, in most cases, it will take you directly to the ball. Paying close attention on crooked shots will save you plenty of golf balls, time, and strokes. In competition, the player may change golf balls either on the tee or if the ball becomes damaged. The ball you put in play must be the same make and model as the one you are taking out of play. In other words, just because the ball is round and white, you may not necessarily put it in play. Have more golf balls than you need and make sure they are the same brand and model. (Tiger Woods stood on the last hole at Pebble Beach during the U.S. Open and, unbeknownst to him, his caddy had no more golf balls left. If Tiger had hit the ball out of play, he would have been unable to finish the round.)

358 TENDING THE FLAGSTICK
Keith Meskic, Tam O'Shanter Club, Brookville, New York

Caddies are often asked to tend the pin, that is, leave the flagstick in the hole and then pull it out after the player has hit the shot or putt. It is mandatory to test this first. Can I easily pull the flagstick out before the player attempts the stroke? Rarely (but it will happen), the flagstick will be stuck in the cup. When the caddy tries to pull the flagstick, the lining of the cup also will come out. The ball will not go in the cup and there will be a penalty. So check to make sure the flagstick can be easily withdrawn before the player hits the shot.

359 THE PLAYER-CADDY TEAM
Keith Meskic, Tam O'Shanter Club, Brookville, New York

The caddy can help in providing yardages, having equipment ready, and so on, but cannot actually save strokes. Yet, as part of the team, he can cost a player strokes if rules are broken. If he breaks the rules—for instance, by moving a player's ball, even accidentally— the player receives the penalty. The caddy should ask the player or an official if he is not certain about a specific rule.

DIFFERENT
TYPES
OF GOLF
COURSES

360 PREPARE FOR THE COURSE

Jay Morelli, Director of the Original Golf School, Mount Snow, Vermont

There are many different types of courses (see the next few pages), and the types and styles of courses are most often defined by the terrain they are built on. Know the terrain you're about to encounter before arriving at the course, and prepare ahead of time for the challenges that lie ahead of you.

361 THE MOUNTAIN COURSE
Jay Morelli, Director of the Original Golf School, Mount Snow, Vermont

There are many different types of courses, and they are usually defined by the terrain they are built on. Mountain courses present a unique challenge—they have uneven lies. In fact, you can hardly find a level lie in a mountain course. The biggest challenge you face is judging how the change in elevation affects club selection. Obviously, the ball will fly a shorter distance uphill with a given club than it will on flat ground. The reverse is also true. The ball will fly farther down the hill than on flat ground. To judge this, your best tool is visualization and imagination. A good rule of thumb is to add or subtract one club for every ten-yard change in elevation. If you have a 150-yard shot uphill, you may need your 160- or 170-yard club. If the 150-yard shot is downhill, you may need to use a 140- or 130-yard club. Experience and imagination, not the yardage book, will be your keys to success.

362 DESERT COURSES
Jay Morelli, Director of the Original Golf School, Mount Snow, Vermont

Desert courses are usually flat and have minimal wind. The challenge with the desert course is normally avoiding the wild shot, as crooked shots normally end up near cacti and snakes. Avoid hazards, be accurate, and go long.

363 LINKS COURSES

Jay Morelli, Director of the Original Golf School, Mount Snow, Vermont

Another style is the links course. By definition, the links course is near water and has few, if any, trees. The challenge with links-style courses is the wind. It's almost a guarantee the wind will blow and low-punch-type shots will be in order.

364 TRADITIONAL COURSES

Jay Morelli, Director of the Original Golf School, Mount Snow, Vermont

The traditional course is one that has many tree-lined holes and does not have too much change in elevation. A good example would be the Winged Foot Golf Club or Bethpage Black Course on Long Island. These courses normally require less local knowledge and fewer specialty shots. While wind is always a factor, it is usually less of a factor on the traditional course as trees will normally protect the course from the type of wind you would experience on a links course.

365 FLORIDA COURSES
Jay Morelli, Director of the Original Golf School, Mount Snow, Vermont

There are unique challenges to playing golf in Florida. The obvious challenge is the wind. There is almost no change in elevation on a Florida course, and the wind can really sweep across the fairways. A key to playing in wind is to control your ball's trajectory. Usually hitting the ball low will give you more control. Another challenge is the grain of the grass on the green. Grass does not grow straight up and down. It tends to grow at an angle—the result being similar to the nap of a rug. The factors that affect which way the grass grows are wind, drainage, and sun. The grain on the greens in Florida normally runs toward the west. The direction of the grain will affect the speed of your putts. If you are putting against the grain, the ball will be slowed down, so you have to hit the ball harder. If you are putting with the grain, the ball will roll with less resistance, and, therefore, you will have to hit the ball with a lighter touch. The grain will also affect the break of the putt. If the grass looks light, you are putting with the grain. If it looks dull, you are putting against the grain.

About the Authors

Jay Morelli is Director of the Original Golf School at Mount Snow, Vermont, and Plantation Golf Resort in Florida. He has been teaching and improving golfers at all skill levels for more than forty years. He founded the Original Golf School and the Accelerated Teaching Method in June 1978. *Golf Digest* voted him the top teaching pro in Vermont, and he has been named New England PGA Teacher of the Year. He has produced four major DVDs and written four books on golf.

Bruce Curtis has been at the forefront of photography for more than four decades. He has chronicled many significant events of the last thirty years. As a photographer for *Time*, *Life*, and *Sports Illustrated*, he has been on the frontlines as a photographer of many conflicts around the world. He has won more than twenty-five awards for his photography and has provided photography for more than forty books.

Acknowledgments

The authors would like to thank the following: all the wonderful teaching pros who contributed to this book, Buffalo Communications, Bill Feidler, Jaime Brooks, David Griffith, Mamiya Golf Shafts, Jared Kelowitz, Jeff Dean, Bridgestone Golf, Inc., Cory Consuegra, Dan Murphy, ECCO, Fila Golf, Nikon, Cleveland Golf, Adams Golf, and Power Built Golf.

Index